I072087

Botanicals

from the

Royal Collection

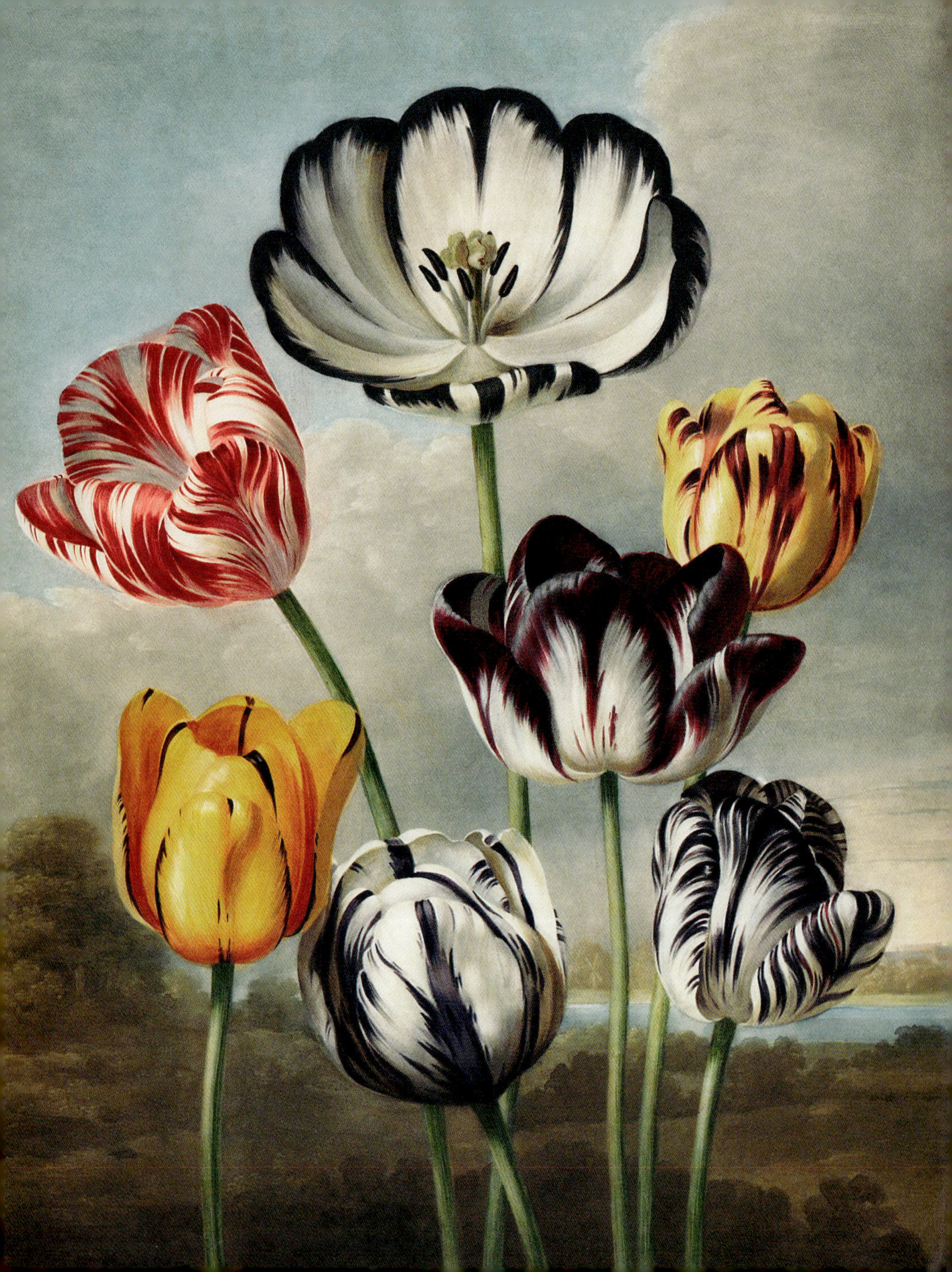

Botanicals

from the
Royal Collection

ROYAL COLLECTION TRUST

Botanicals from the Royal Collection

The natural world has been of great interest to royalty for centuries, from the menageries of medieval kings, the kitchen and physic gardens of the Tudor and Stuart monarchs and the aviaries and botanical gardens of the Georgians and Victorians through to His Majesty King Charles III's own initiatives to support biodiversity, sustainability and the environment today. As a result, the Royal Collection is brimming with beautiful examples of natural history art assembled by generations of royal collectors.

The botanical drawings included here all reflect artists' extraordinary engagement with the natural world and skill in depicting it. Many are taken from four groups of material in the Royal Collection, dating from the seventeenth or early eighteenth centuries: Alexander Marshal's watercolours of plants growing in English gardens, Maria Sibylla Merian's illustrations of insects and plants in Suriname, Mark Catesby's studies of American flora and fauna, and the precise botanical studies drawn to assist the investigations of Roman collector and scientist Cassiano dal Pozzo.

Cassiano dal Pozzo (1588–1657) was a member of the Accademia dei Lincei, the first scientific academy in Europe. The members of this 'Academy of the Lynxes' – named after the fabled eyesight of that animal – emphasised observation as key to the study of nature: nothing could be assumed unless it had been seen and recorded. Driven by this documentary impulse, Cassiano assembled a 'paper museum' of prints and drawings, building a lucid record of the natural world. Cassiano did not produce these rigorous drawings himself: he commissioned artists – their identities mostly unknown to us – and acquired artworks from other collections. In 1762, the Paper Museum was, in turn, bought by an avid collector of natural history – George III.

The clarity of Cassiano's drawings reflects their scientific purpose. The same specimen is typically shown from multiple angles. The artists include seed heads and roots beside the main bodies of plants. Fruit is split into segments to allow the viewer to understand the internal structure: the pomelo, a fruit praised for its enormous size, is shown to be mainly pith. The Paper Museum also contained depictions of deformed plants, including an enormous head of broccoli and an orange 'pregnant' with another smaller fruit. By examining abnormal specimens, Cassiano and his contemporaries hoped to explain the mechanics of reproduction.

Cassiano also acquired living and preserved specimens. His drawings allowed him to expand the scope of his collection beyond what was easily obtainable, and to draw attention to particular characteristics of plants and animals. Living plants can wither, dried specimens change colour, and written descriptions can be misunderstood. Cassiano's drawings provided stable reference points for those attempting to organise and categorise the natural world.

The function of botanical illustration as a permanent record of transient plants is demonstrated nowhere more beautifully than in the work of Alexander Marshal (1620–82), who vividly captures flowers that bloomed in seventeenth-century London. Marshal was part of a circle of horticulturalists who exchanged plants and seeds to create gardens rich in diversity and beauty. Over 30 years Marshal compiled a *florilegium* (flower book) illustrating

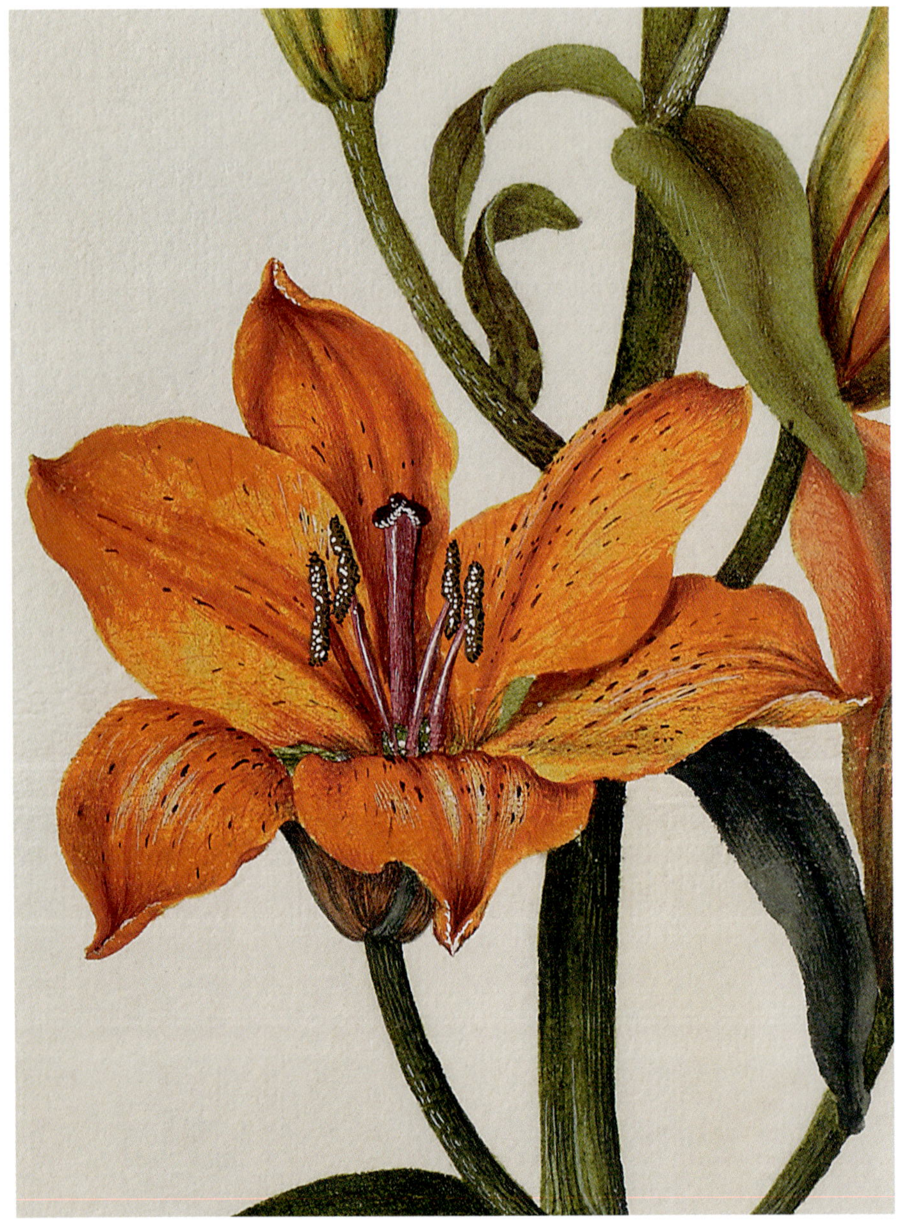

284 species of plant growing in his and his acquaintances' gardens. Marshal broadly organised these drawings by season, from winter snowdrops, to blowsy summer roses, to the bright autumnal berries of a Chinese lantern. Contemporaries praised Marshal's artistic talent but, despite the *florilegium*'s renown, it was not intended for publication or sale. Instead, it was a labour of love, to be studied and enjoyed by Marshal, his friends and circle of fellow gardeners. After Marshal's death, his *florilegium* remained with his family for some years before being sold. It was eventually presented to George IV in the 1820s.

The pleasure Marshal derived from painting plants is evident. These are not generalised depictions, but meticulous 'portraits' resulting from careful observation. Marshal lovingly picked out the veins in irises' petals or the fine hairs of a poppy's stem with delicate brushstrokes. He resisted the urge to perfect blemished leaves or repair insect damage, giving an impression of an unforced, minutely observed reality.

Like Cassiano's artists, Marshal positioned his subjects to present their botanical structures most effectively. He depicted the stamen and pistils of a great orange lily and showed its flowers from different angles and stages of development, from bud to full bloom. His compositions are varied and lively. On one sheet he

Great orange lily

Alexander Marshal,
*c.*1650–82

RCIN 924362

Mourning iris

Alexander Marshal,
*c.*1650–82

RCIN 924325

artfully arranged 14 striped auriculas, on another he played with scale, perching a miniature goldfinch on the leaf of a sunflower.

Inscriptions in Marshal's hand identify many of the plants he drew. Like the 'trew figure of Ginger as it grew att Fulham', many were recent imports to English shores. Feathered and flamed tulips, ripening chillies and the spectacular crown imperial, all newcomers from overseas, are shown beside plants native to English fields and hedgerows. The variety of plant species available to a European gardener expanded during the seventeenth century, the result of European trade with, and exploration and colonisation of, the Americas, Africa and south-east Asia.

Collectors and artists experienced the Americas through seeds and specimens painstakingly brought back from overseas, and some travelled to encounter plants in their natural habitats. One such artist was Maria Sibylla Merian (1647–1717). Merian was born in Frankfurt, where her stepfather, the still-life artist Jacob Marrel, taught her to paint flowers in watercolour. Alongside this artistic education, Merian developed an enduring interest in entomology. Between 1679 and 1683, she published two volumes on the insect life cycle, the product of years of careful study.

By 1665, Merian was living in Amsterdam. Seventeenth-century Holland was a major colonial power, and Amsterdam its wealthy, trading heart. Ships arrived in the city daily, carrying plants and animals from the Americas, Asia and Africa – cargo that fuelled the research of scholars keen to collect and categorise new specimens. Merian visited their collections of natural curiosities, and 'saw with wonderment the beautiful creatures brought back from the East and West Indies'. But preserved specimens could not advance Merian's understanding of insects: she needed to see them in their natural habitat. In 1699, she set sail to Dutch-controlled Suriname, on the north-east coast of South America.

In Suriname, Merian studied insects and plants in the garden of her house in Paramaribo, in the sugar plantations of Dutch enslavers, and in rainforests 'densely overgrown with thistles and thorn bushes'. Although her primary interest in plants was as food sources for insects, she noted their medicinal and culinary use and potential as building materials. Other Dutch colonists did not share this approach – they were unable to tell Merian the 'name or properties' of a plant growing in her garden and mocked her for 'looking for other things than sugar in the country'.

Instead, Merian relied on the help and knowledge of the Indigenous population of Suriname. Studying the specimens they supplied to her, she described how they used plants as medicine, food and insect repellents. She also documented the botanical knowledge of enslaved African labourers and the terrible conditions they endured. But Merian also benefitted from enslaved labour: when embarking on an expedition into the rainforest, she sent her 'slaves ahead with axe in hand' to hack a path through the dense undergrowth.

After contracting a weakening illness – possibly malaria – Merian returned to Holland in 1701, laden with specimens, field notes and sketches. She worked her research up into a beautifully illustrated book, *Metamorphosis Insectorum Surinamensium* ('The Transformations of the Insects of Suriname'), published in 1705 in Amsterdam. Merian's hand-coloured illustrations showed insects interacting with the plants that sustained them – an innovative approach as flora and fauna were typically illustrated separately.

It is easy to imagine the excitement felt by an eighteenth-century reader leafing through the *Metamorphosis*. Merian's delight with the plants she encountered is tangible in her work: in the whirling tendrils of a passionflower, the impossibly bright colours of the banana branch, the waxy shine of the watermelon's skin and description of how its flesh 'melted in the mouth like sugar'. Alongside these published illustrations, Merian produced at least two deluxe versions. The set now in the Royal Collection may have been presented to George III, then Prince of Wales, in 1755.

Merian's pioneering depiction of the interconnected relationship between plants and insects had a lasting impact on how others illustrated the natural world. Her influence can be seen in the work of Mark Catesby (1682–1749). Catesby was a Suffolk-born naturalist, and, like Merian, was driven by a 'passionate Desire' to encounter plants 'in their native countries'. Sponsored by a group of patrons, Catesby travelled to North America in 1722 to illustrate the plants and animals of the continent. Catesby arrived in Charleston, Carolina – an area 'abounding in Variety of the Blessings of Nature' and a 'profusion of ... beautiful plants'. He spent his first year on the coastal plain, before making several expeditions up the Savannah River to less inhabited regions, where he was delighted to find species he had not seen before.

Like the other artists in this book, Catesby prioritised close observation. He worked from freshly gathered specimens and plants and animals in the field, making pen and ink sketches with quick colour notes. These formed the basis of larger watercolours executed on his return from expeditions. Catesby described the resulting watercolours as 'Flat, tho' exact', a style chosen to best 'serve the purpose of Natural History'. Catesby captures his subjects with remarkable clarity, showing magnolia seeds suspended by thin threads or the delicate concave flowers of a mountain laurel.

Snapdragon
Collection of Cassiano
dal Pozzo, *c.*1610
RCIN 927788

It is impossible to separate Catesby from British trade in enslaved peoples – Catesby's patrons in Carolina were plantation owners who used enslaved labour – and colonial expansion into the Americas. Like Merian, Catesby was reliant on the 'Hospitality and Assistance' and botanical knowledge of an Indigenous population. He was accompanied on his expeditions by Native Americans and employed an unidentified man 'to carry my Box, in which, besides Paper and Materials for Painting, I put dry'd Specimens of Plants, Seeds, &c'.

In 1725, Catesby travelled to the Bahamas, studying plants and tropical fish, before returning to England. Back in London, he set to work publishing his observations in *The Natural History of Carolina, Florida, and the Bahama Islands* – his drawings formed the basis for the publication's exquisite printed illustrations. These drawings, which transported the flora of the Americas across the Atlantic, were purchased by George III some years after Catesby's death.

Catesby valued his drawings for their 'truth and accuracy'. These qualities resulted from his passionate engagement with the natural world, a passion seen in the work of all the artists included in this book. They all looked curiously at the plants they encountered, whether hollyhocks flowering in a garden by the Thames, snapdragons and foxgloves in Italian fields, okra in Suriname or pitch apples in the Bahamas. Centuries later, their drawings still encourage us to look at the natural world with the same delight.

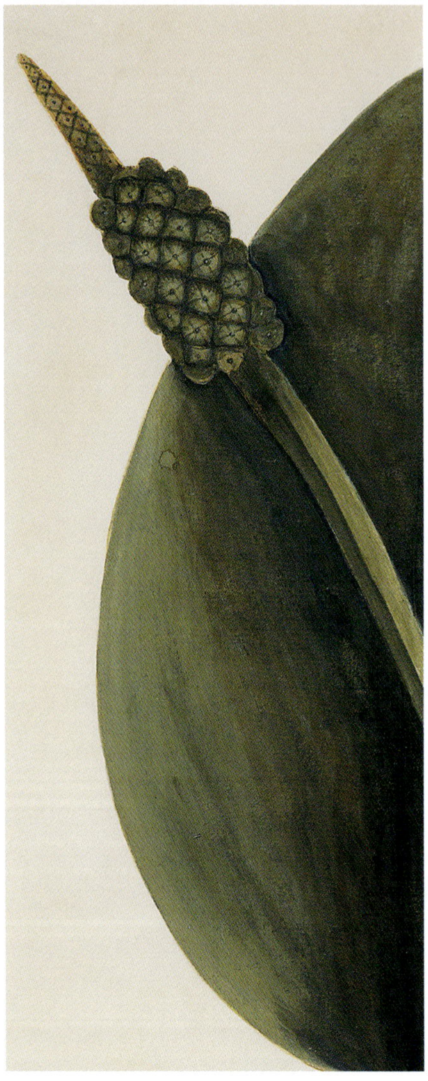

Goldenclub (detail)

Mark Catesby, *c.*1722–6

RCIN 925917

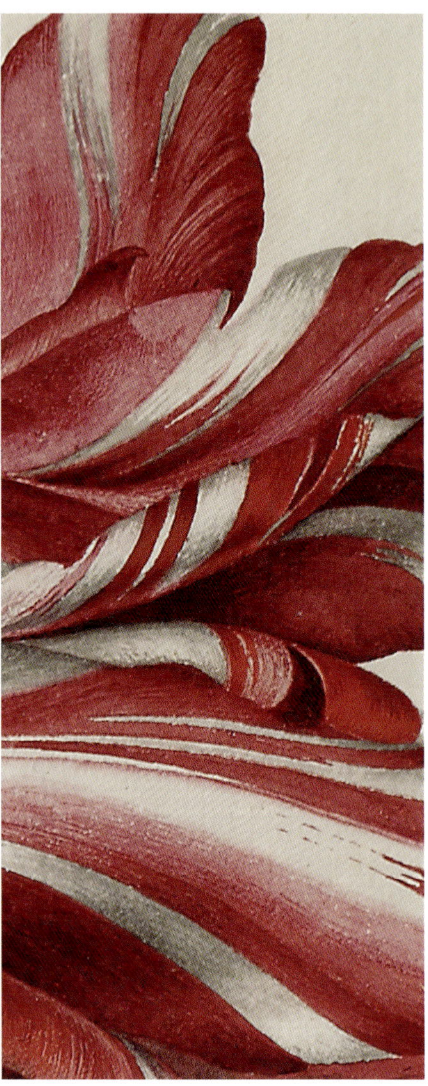

Tulip (detail)

Alexander Marshal, *c.*1680

RCIN 924303

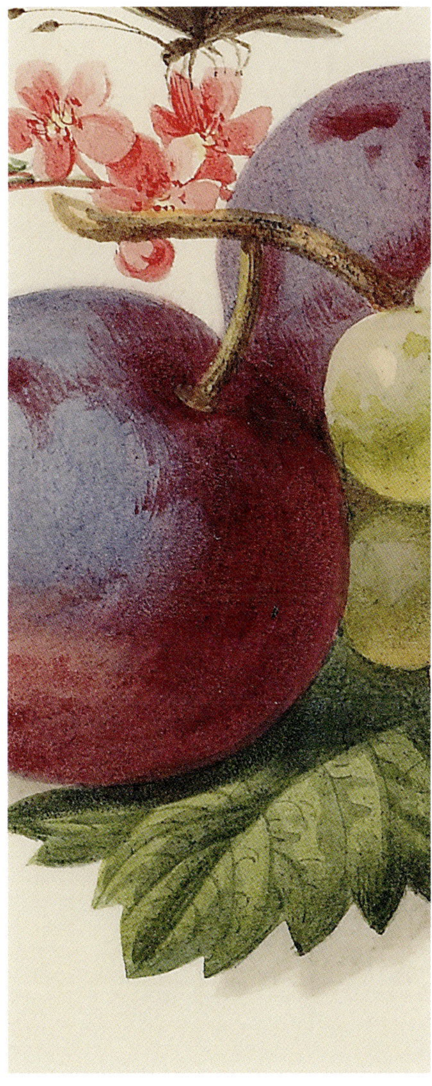

Plums, apple, grapes, a butterfly
and blossom (detail)

Anonymous, *c.*1880

RCIN 931927

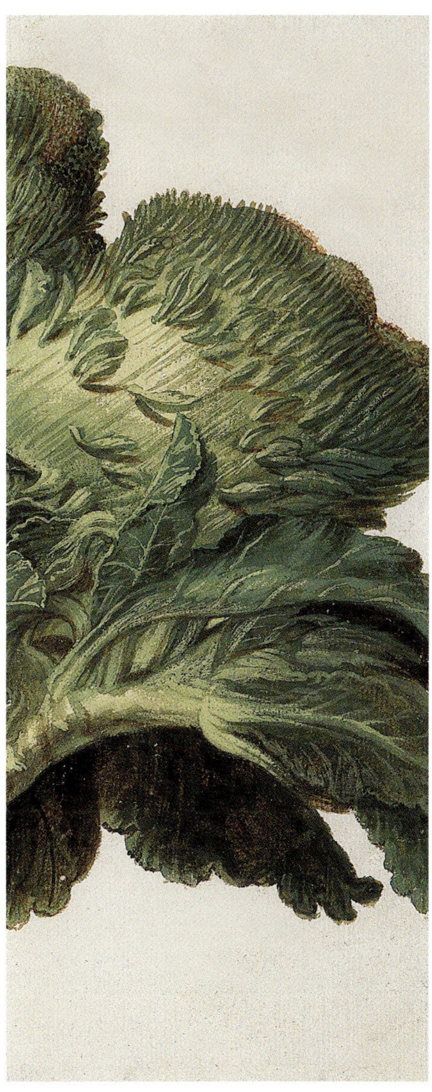

Broccoli (detail)

Collection of Cassiano
dal Pozzo, *c.*1650

RCIN 921143

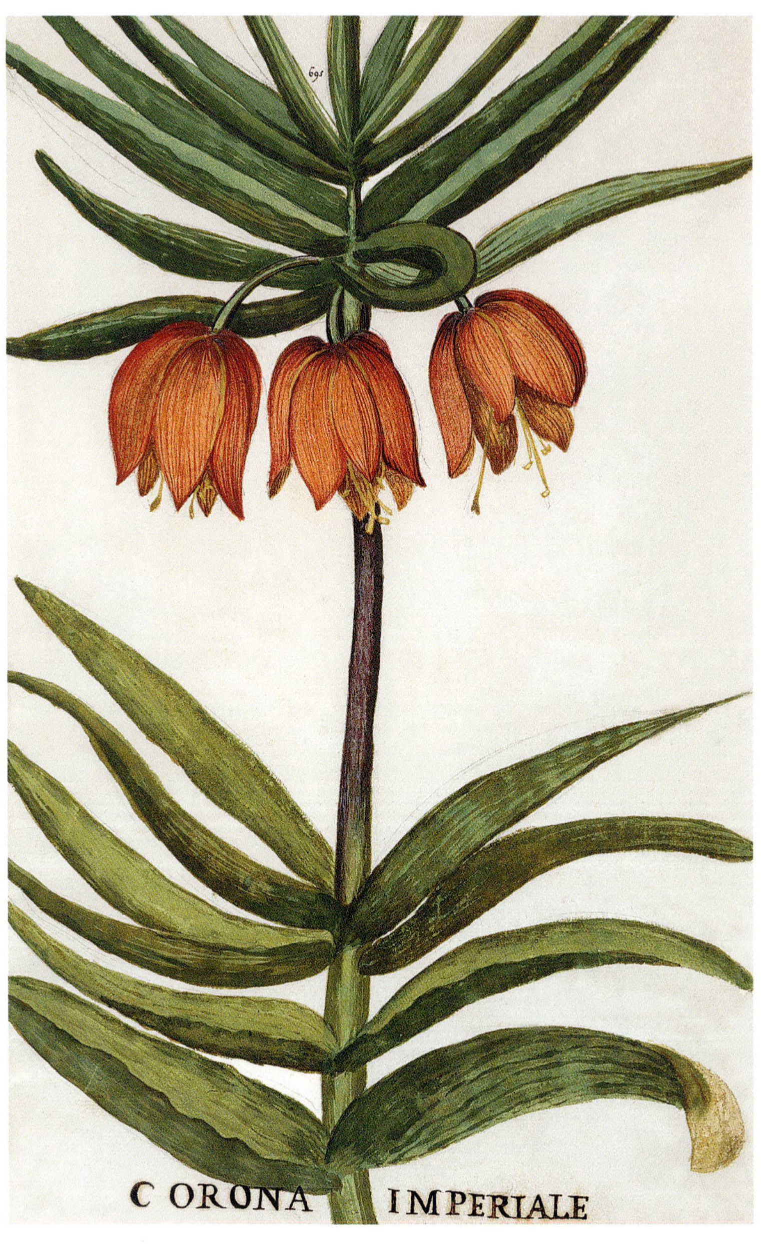

Crown imperial

Collection of
Cassiano dal
Pozzo, *c.*1600–20

RCIN 927890

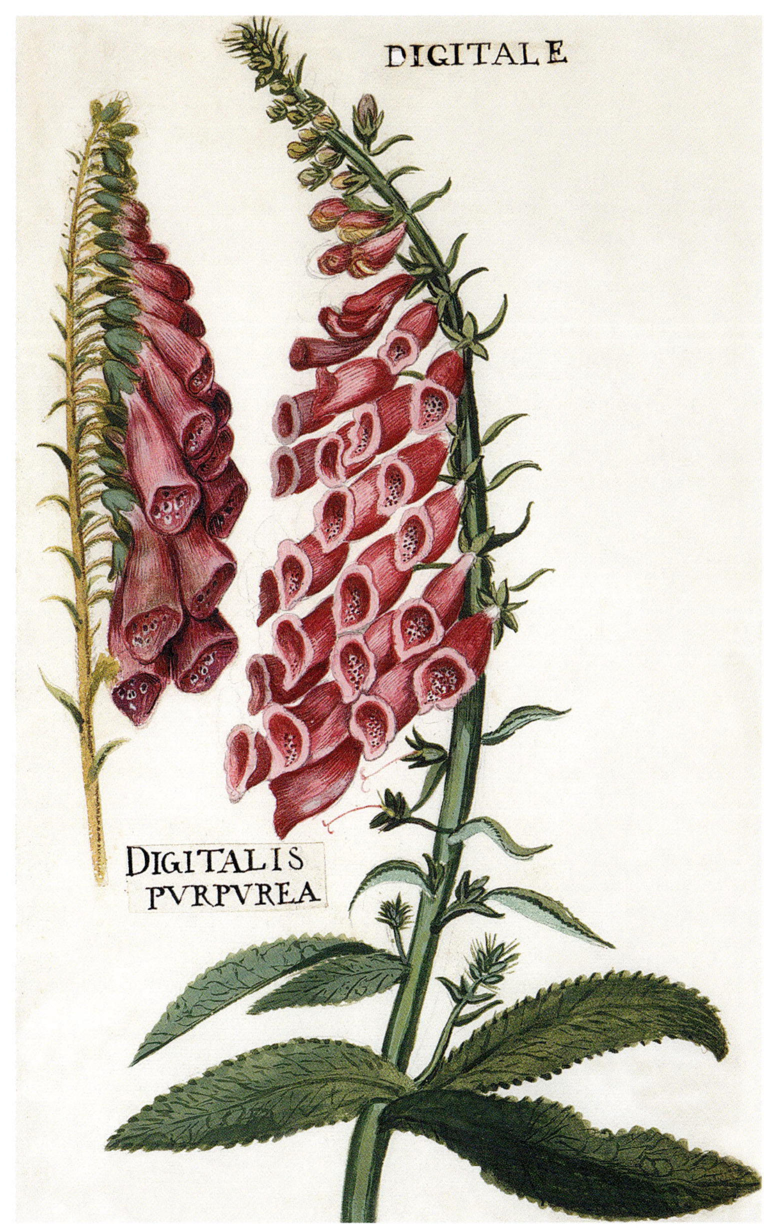

Foxglove

Collection of
Cassiano dal
Pozzo, *c.*1600–20

RCIN 927891

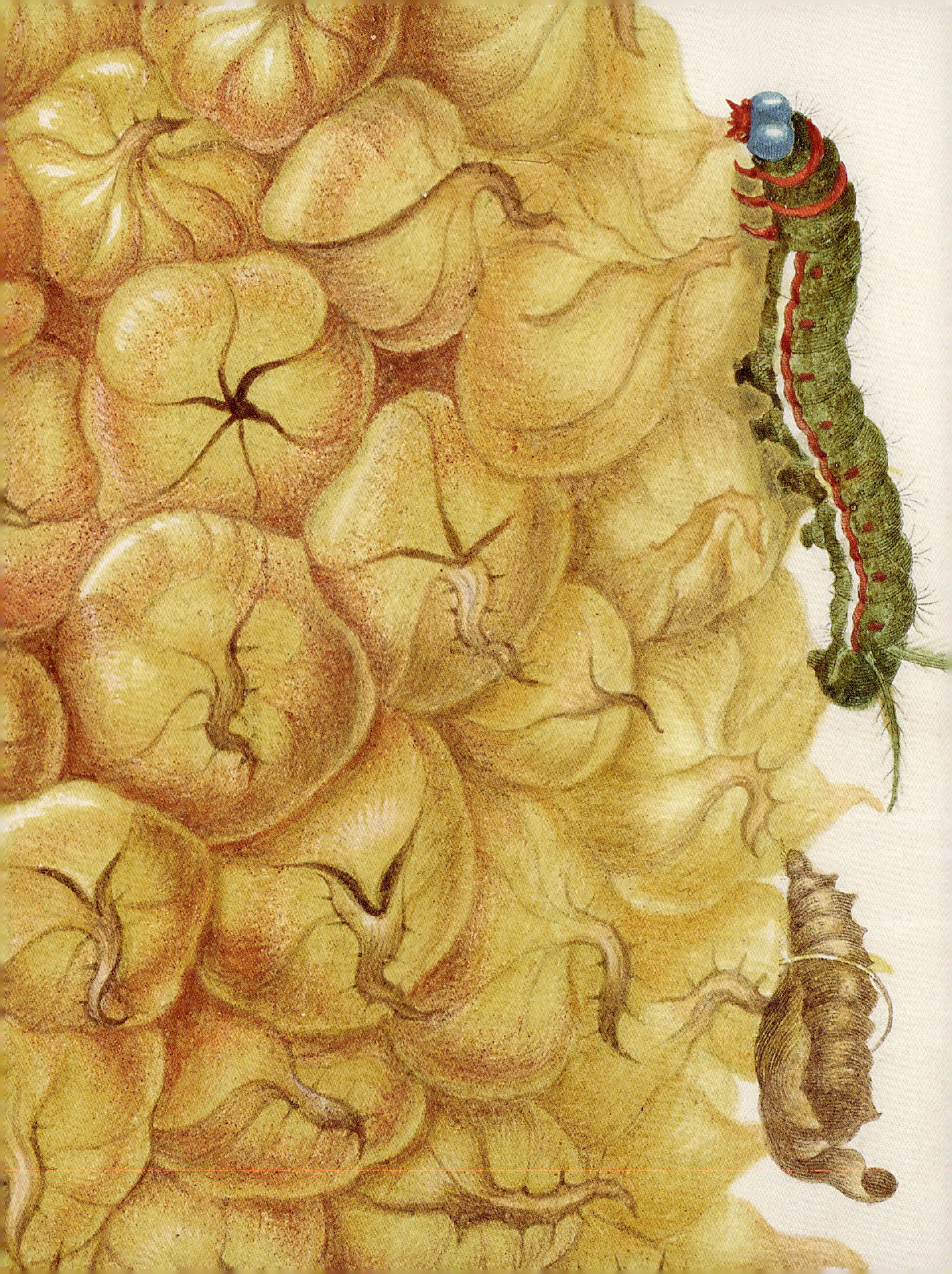

OPPOSITE

Ripe pineapple with dido longwing (detail)

Maria Sibylla
Merian, 1702–3

RCIN 921154

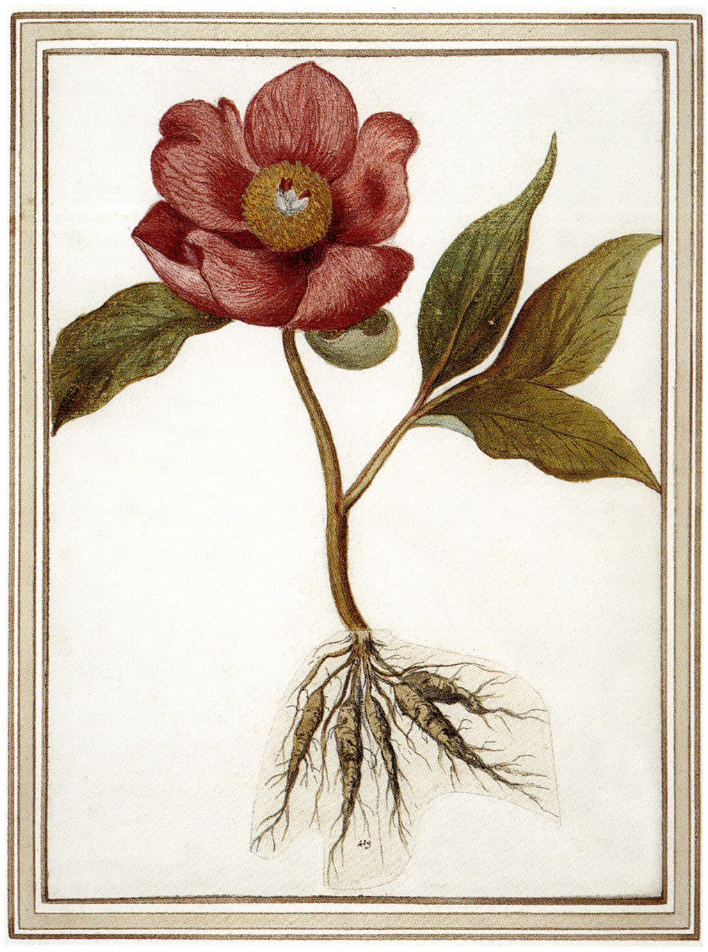

Peony

Collection of
Cassiano dal Pozzo,
c.1610–20

RCIN 919401

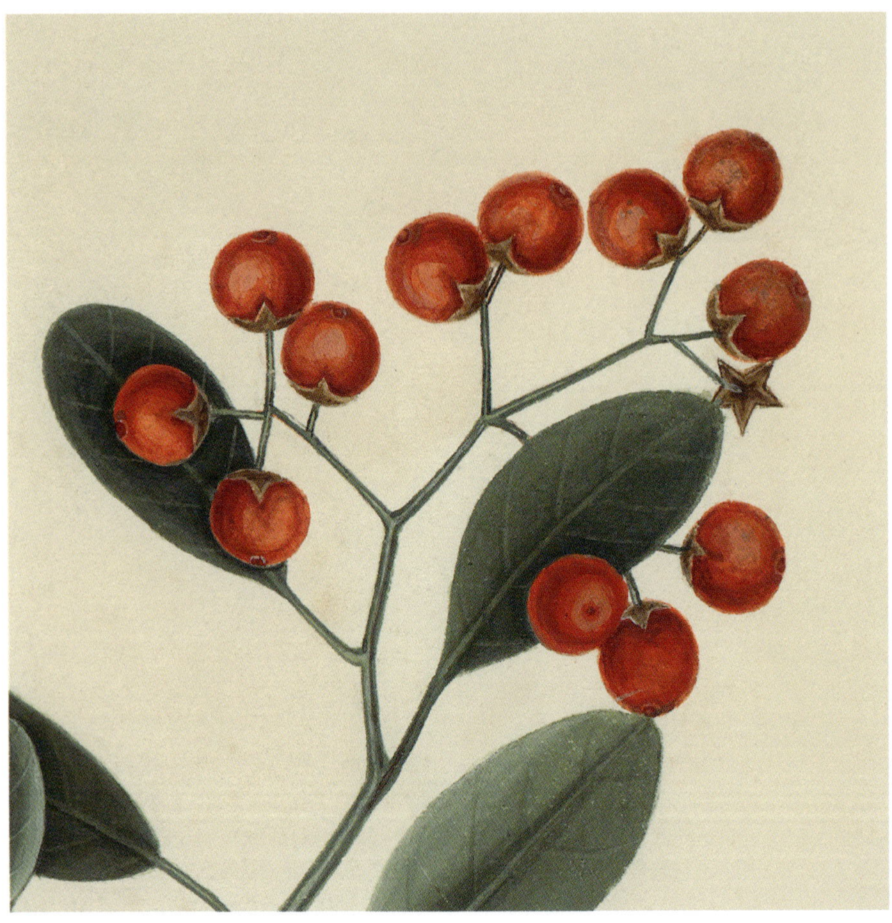

Bodywood (detail)

Mark Catesby,
*c.*1722–6

**Branch of pomelo
with green-banded
urania moth**

Maria Sibylla
Merian, 1702–3

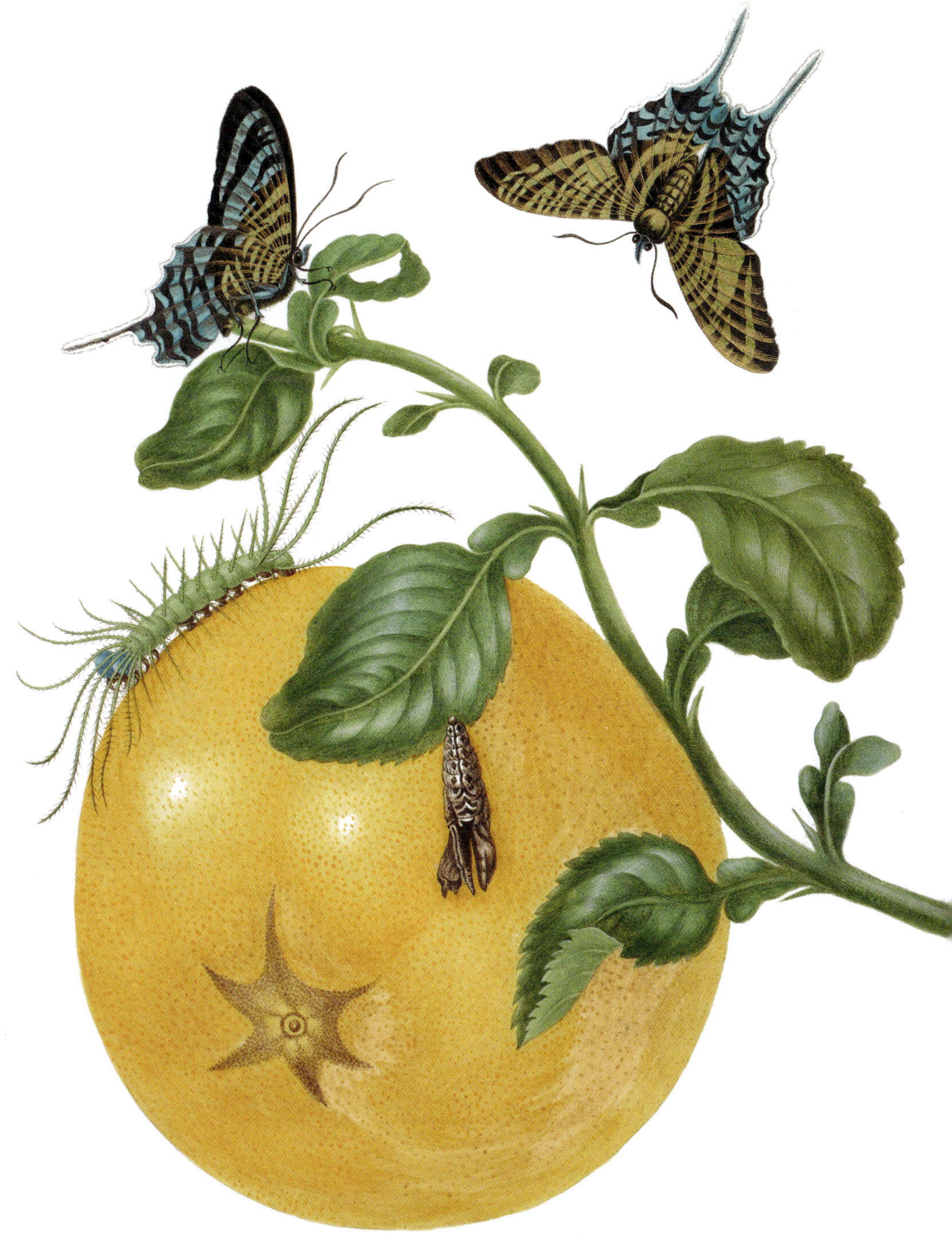

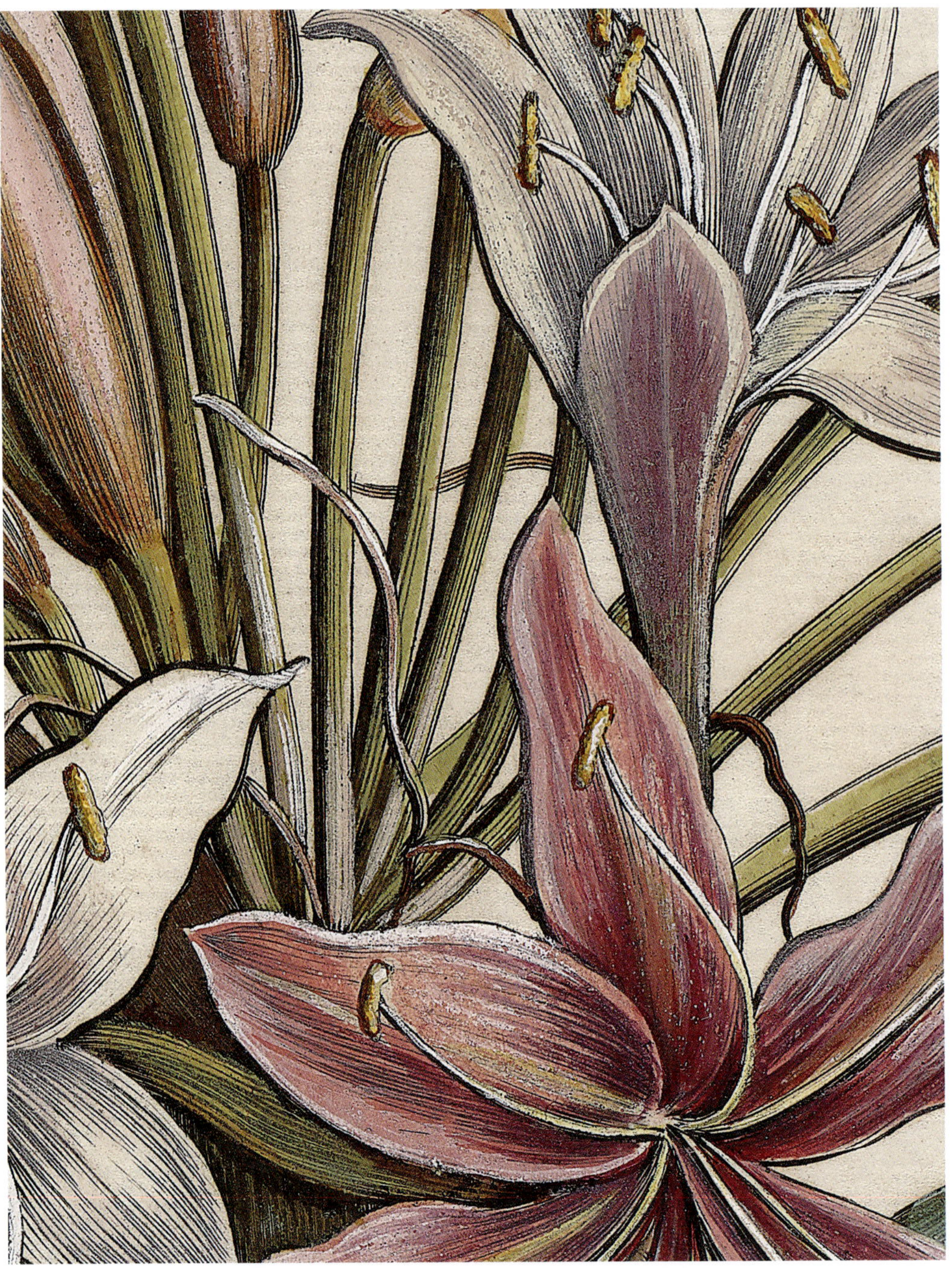

OPPOSITE

Ammocharis longifolia (detail)

From Jan Commelin,
Horti medici Amstelodamensis,
1697

RCIN 1057108

Citron-lemon

Collection of
Cassiano dal
Pozzo, 1626–46

RCIN 919364

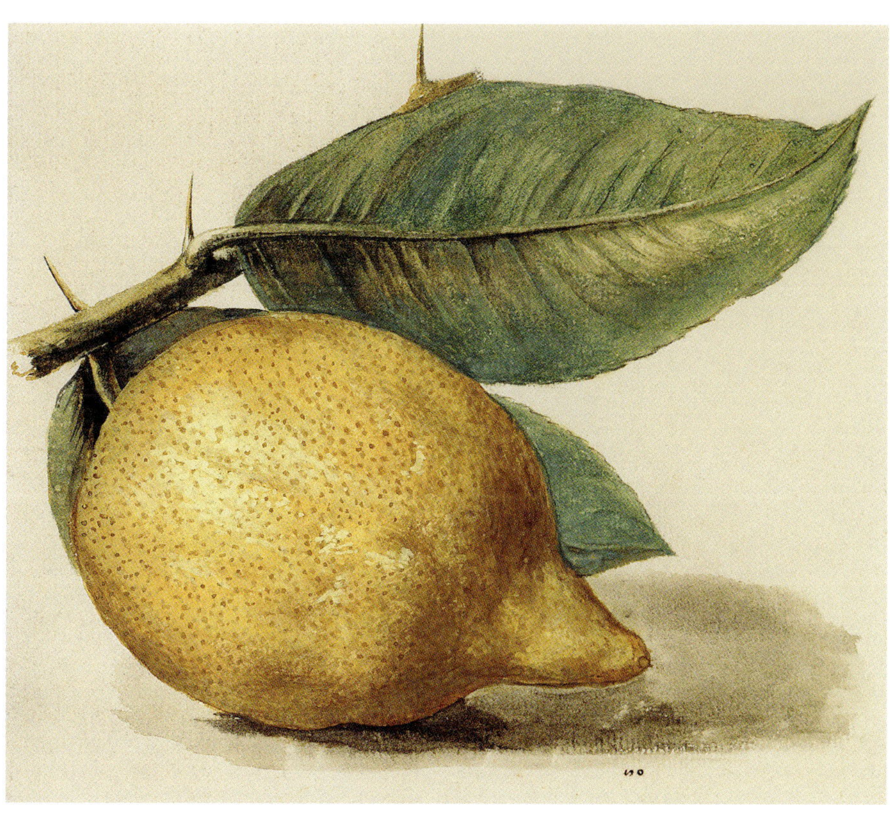

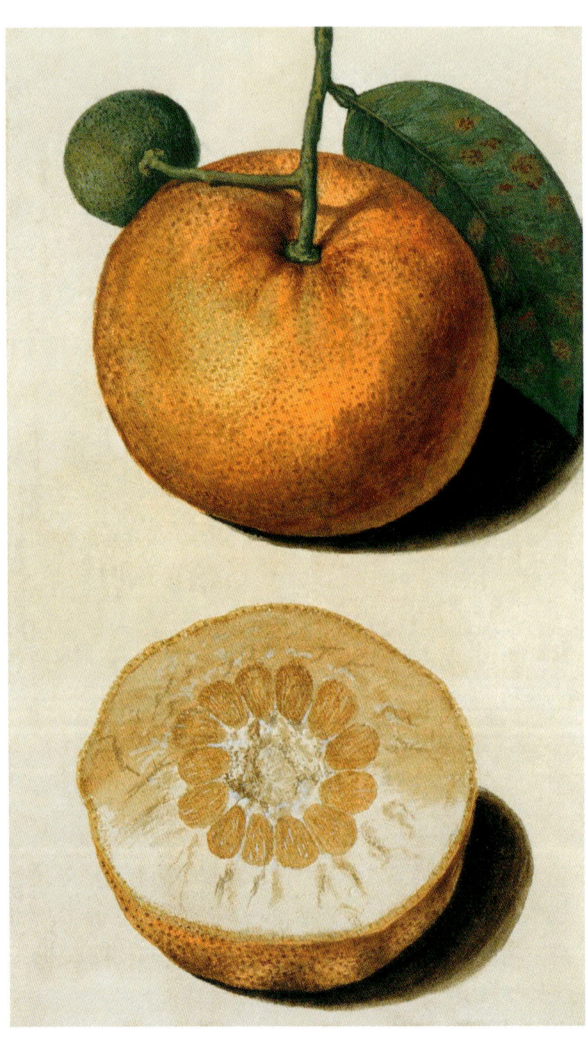

Tievine and geiger-tree

Mark Catesby, *c.*1722–6

RCIN 926054

Pomelo

Collection of Cassiano dal Pozzo, *c.*1640

RCIN 919333

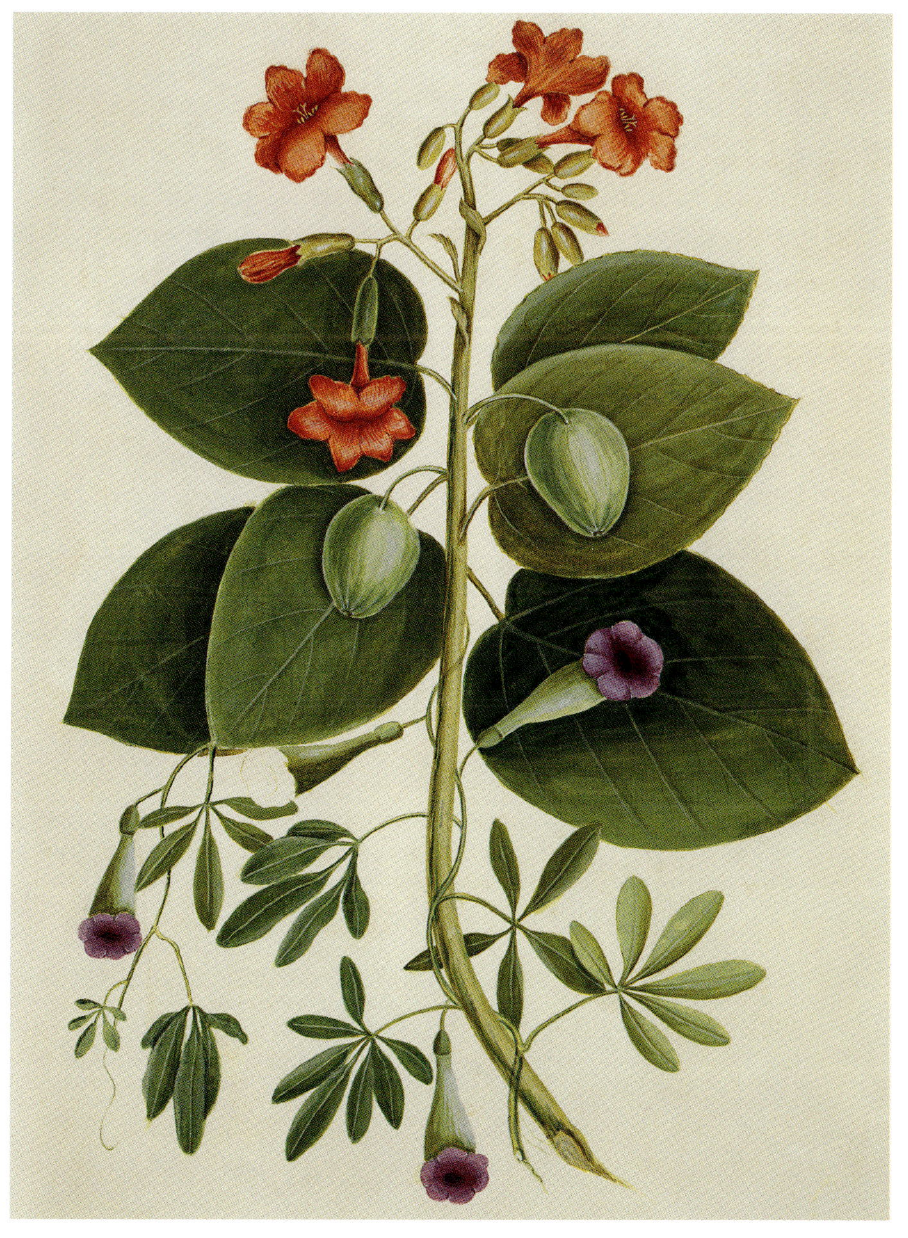

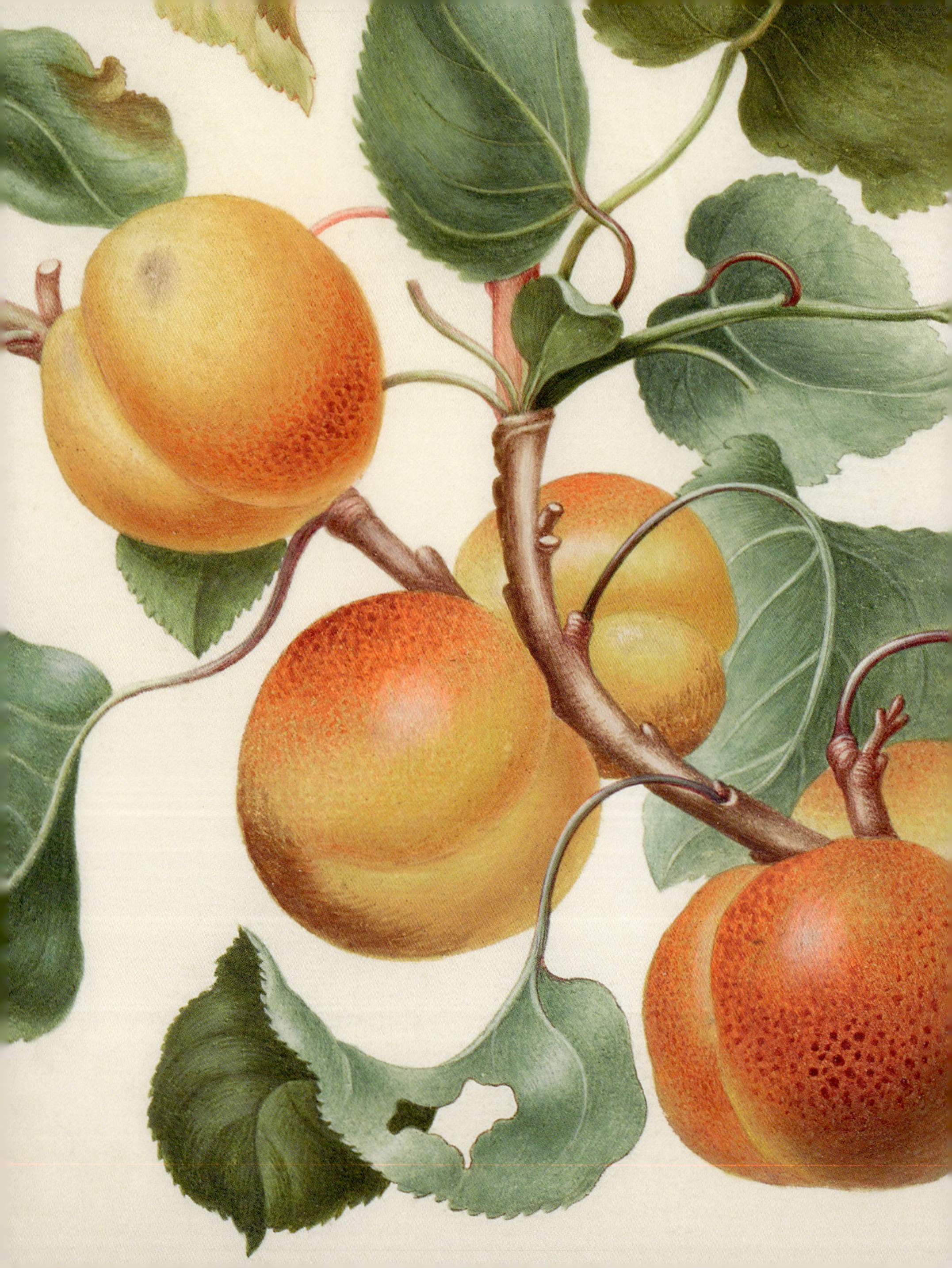

Apricot branch
(detail)

Maria Sibylla
Merian, *c*.1705

RCIN 921231

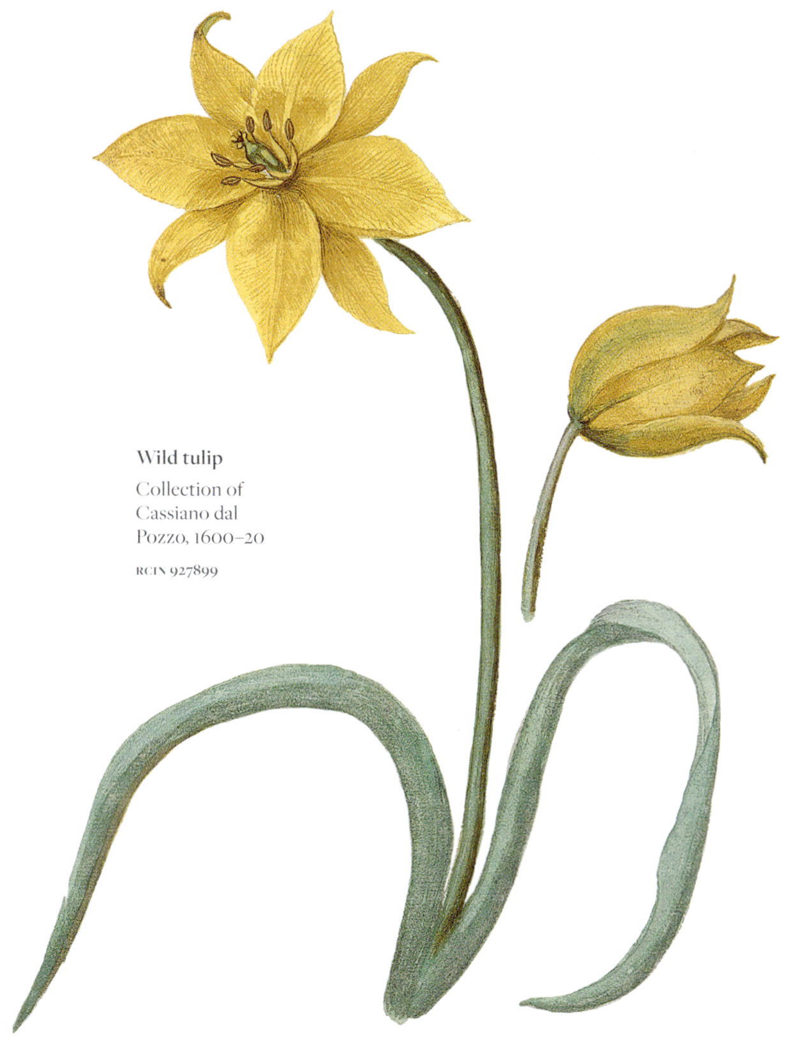

Wild tulip

Collection of
Cassiano dal
Pozzo, 1600–20

RCIN 927899

Cocoa tree with southern armyworm moth (detail)

Maria Sibylla Merian, 1702–3

RCIN 921183

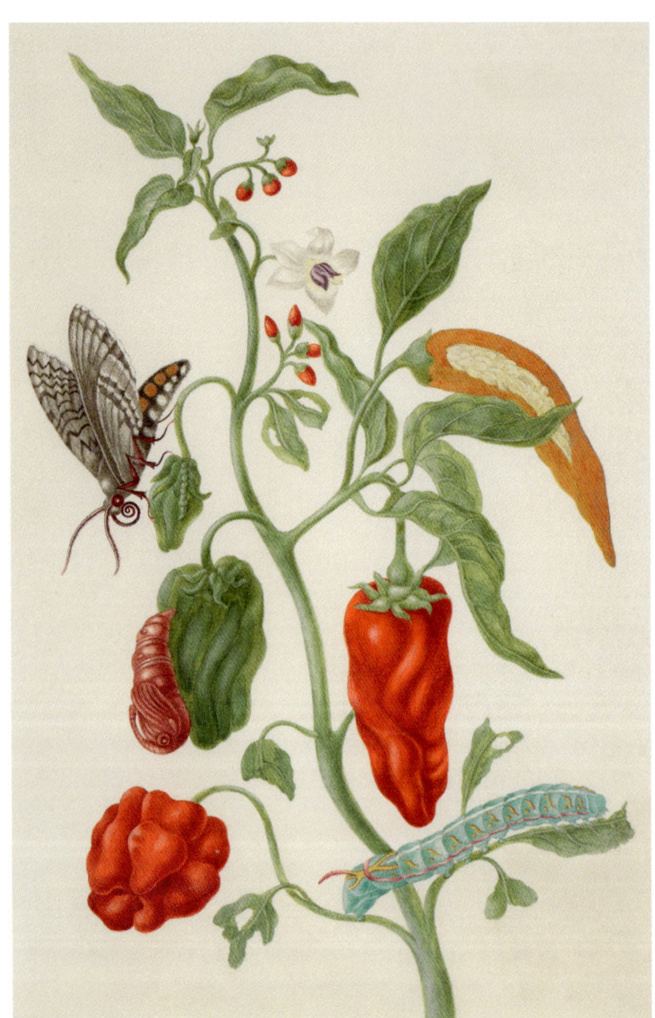

Pepper plant with carolina sphinx moth

Maria Sibylla Merian, 1702–3

RCIN 921212

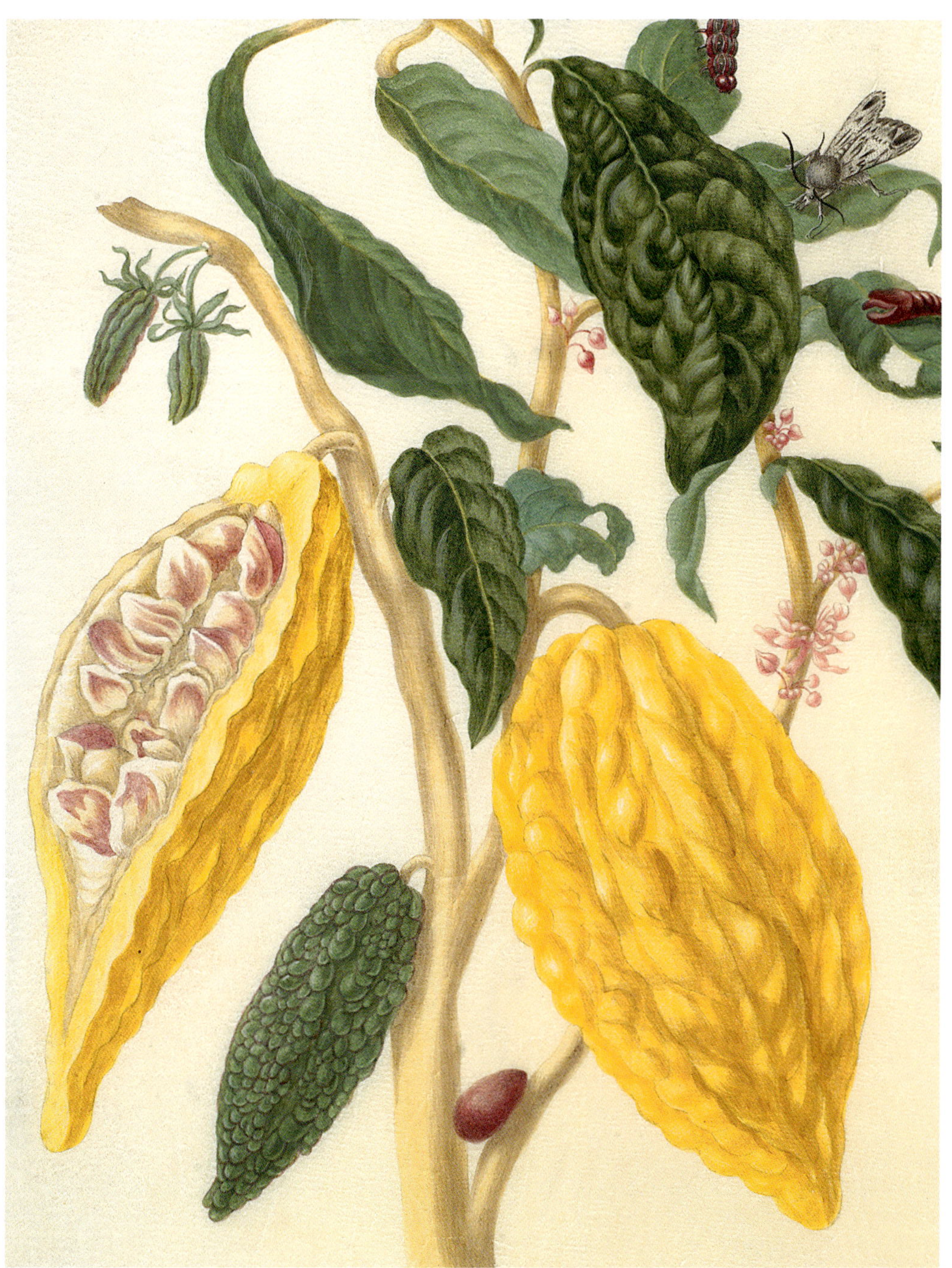

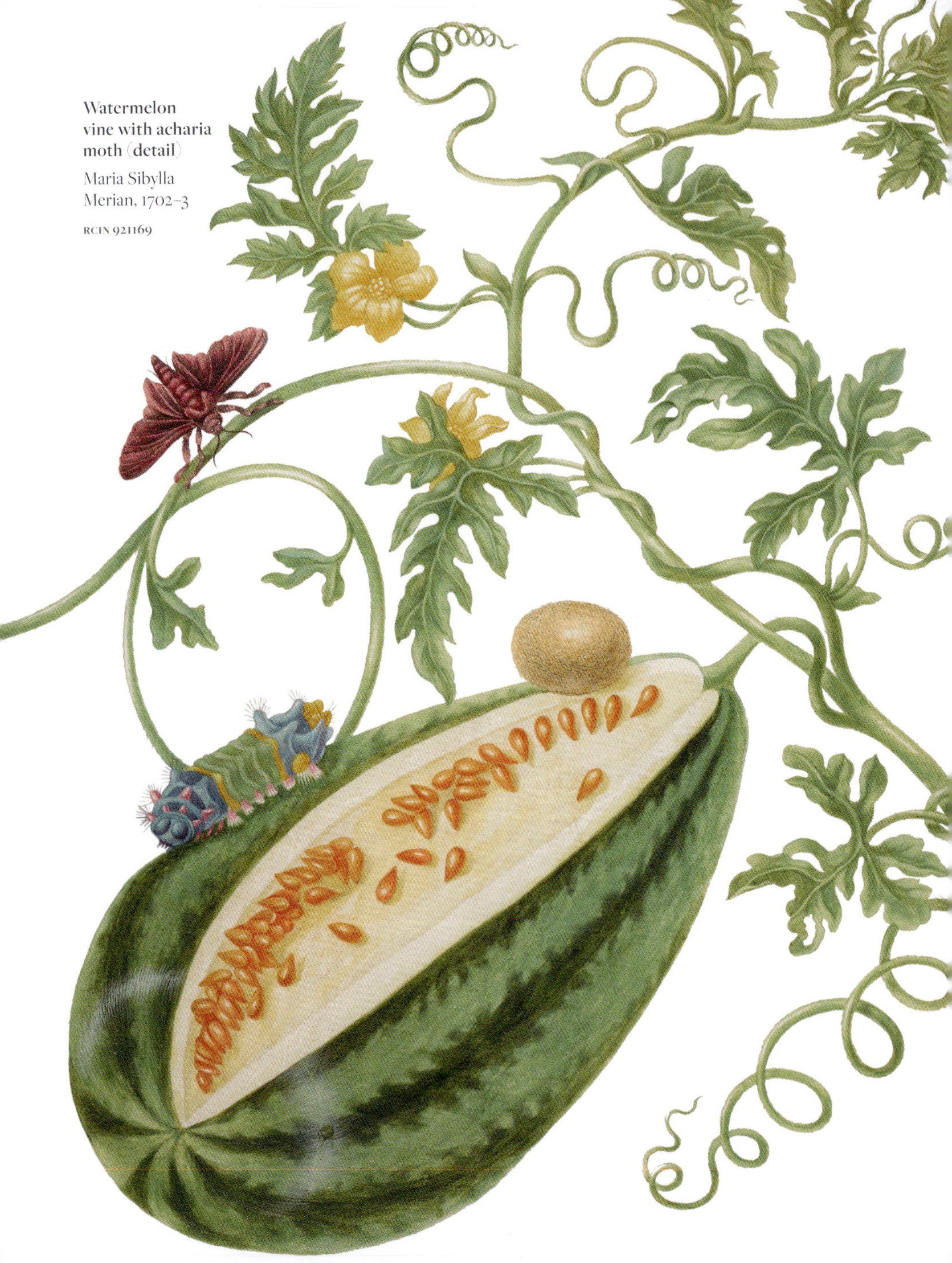

Watermelon
vine with acharia
moth (detail)
Maria Sibylla
Merian, 1702–3
RCIN 921169

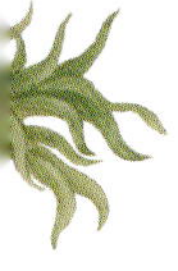

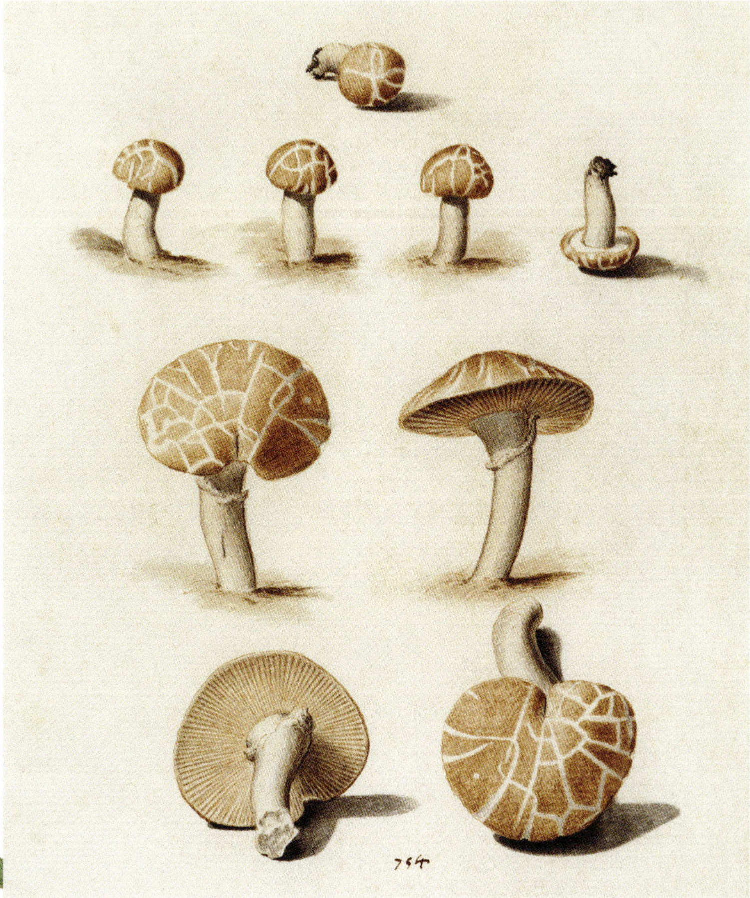

Fungi

Collection of
Cassiano dal
Pozzo, *c*.1650

RCIN 919369

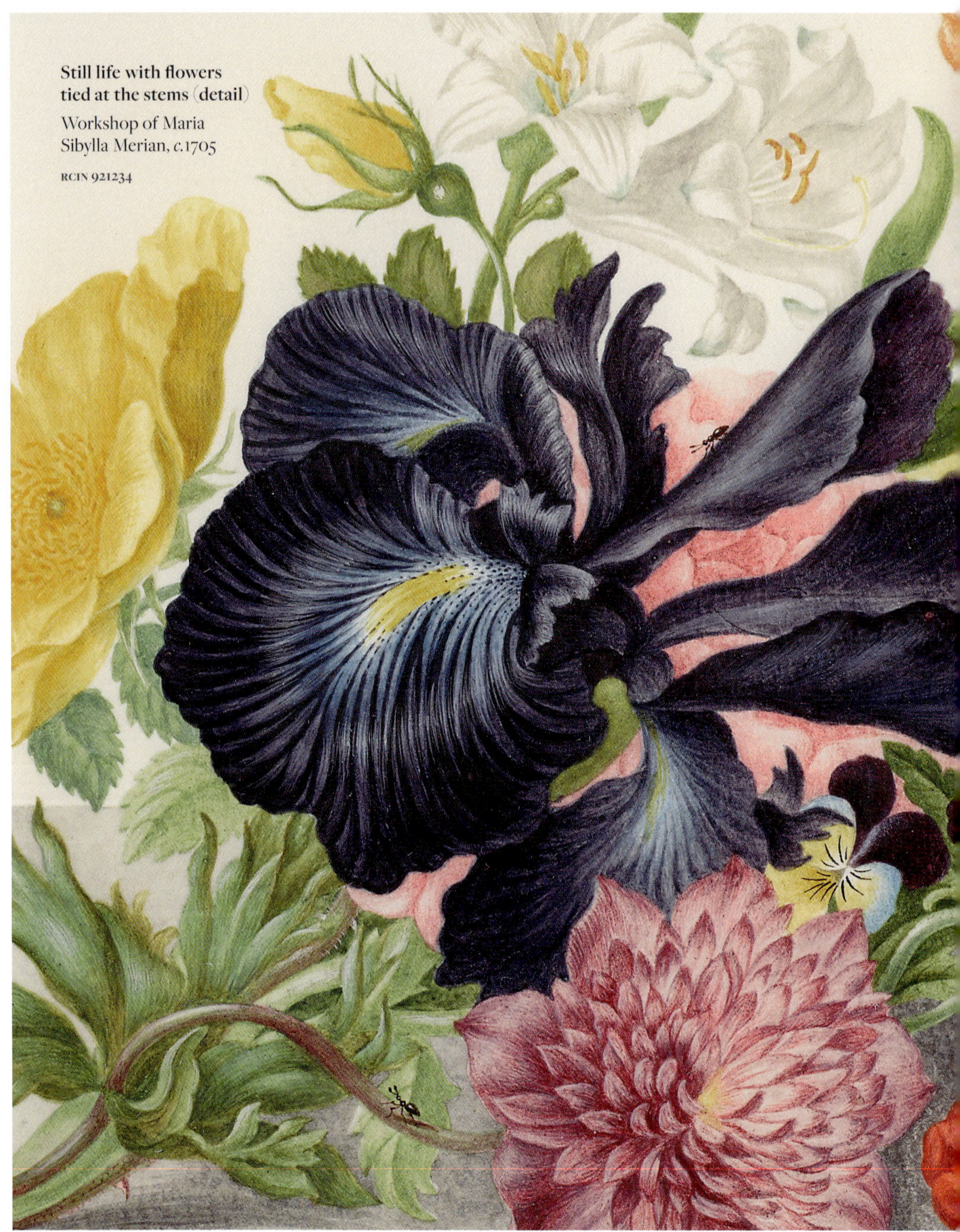

Still life with flowers
tied at the stems (detail)
Workshop of Maria
Sibylla Merian, c.1705
RCIN 921234

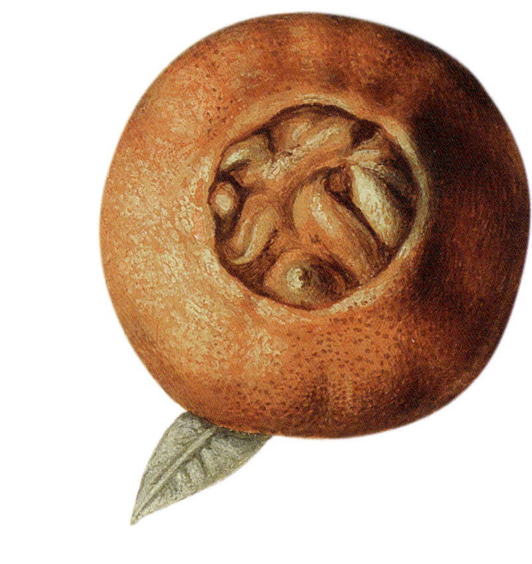

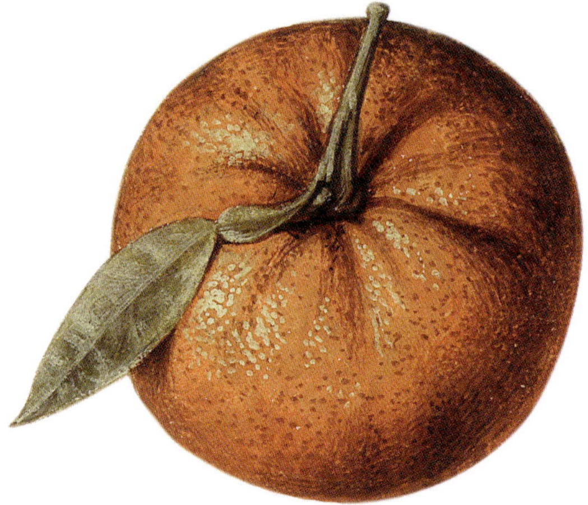

Passionflower (detail)

Maria Sibylla Merian, *c.*1705

RCIN 921176

Sweet orange

Collection of Cassiano dal Pozzo, 1626–46

RCIN 921146

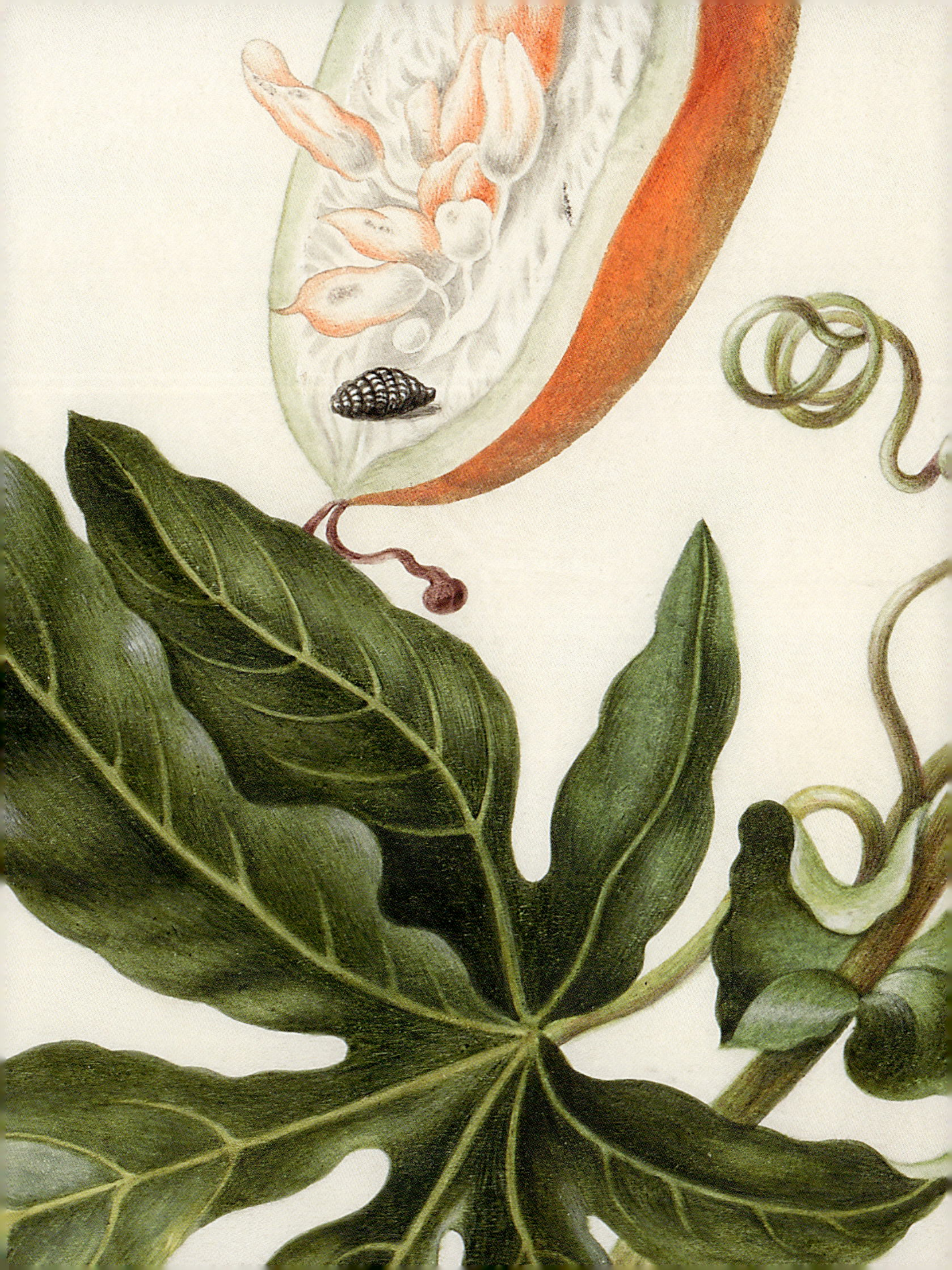

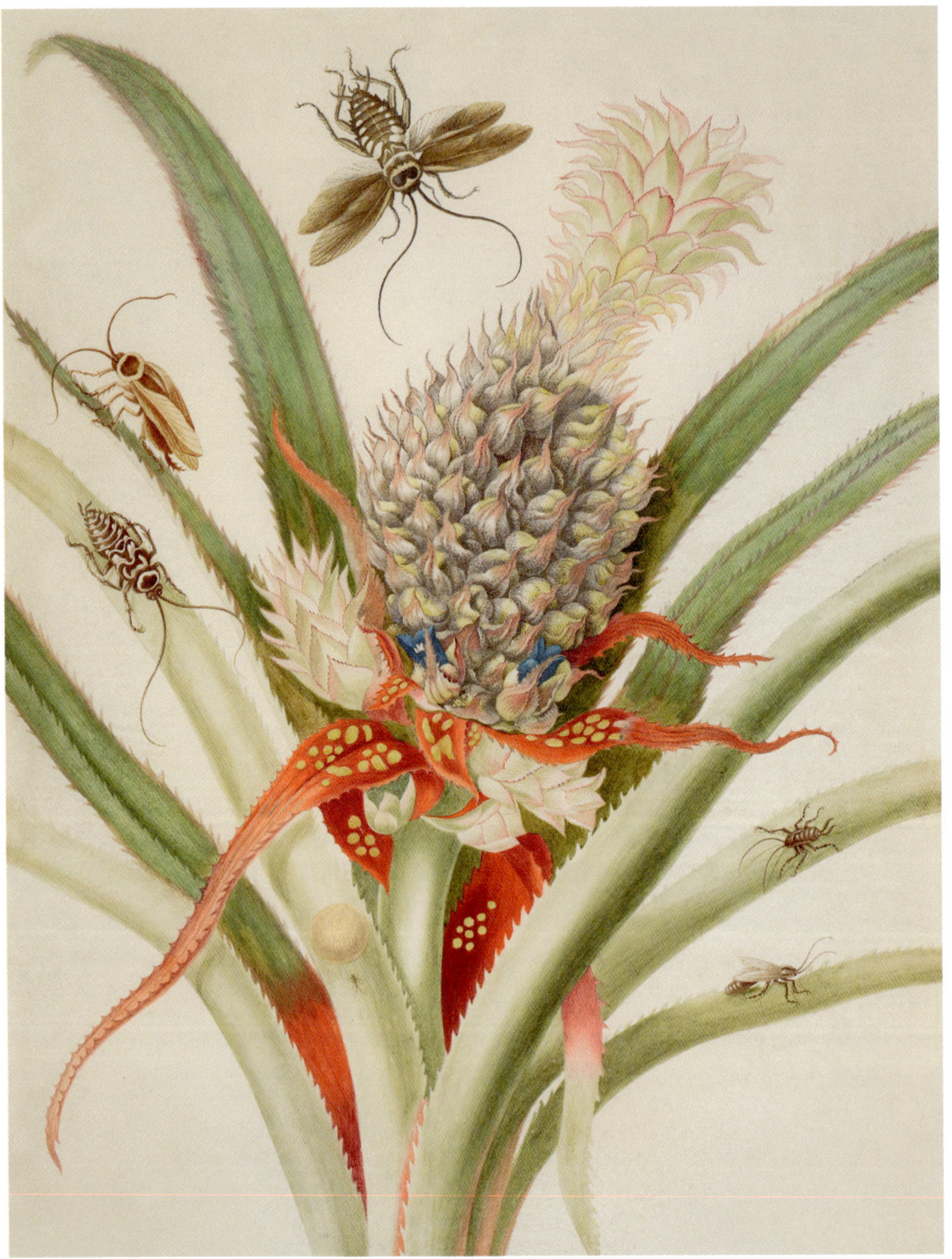

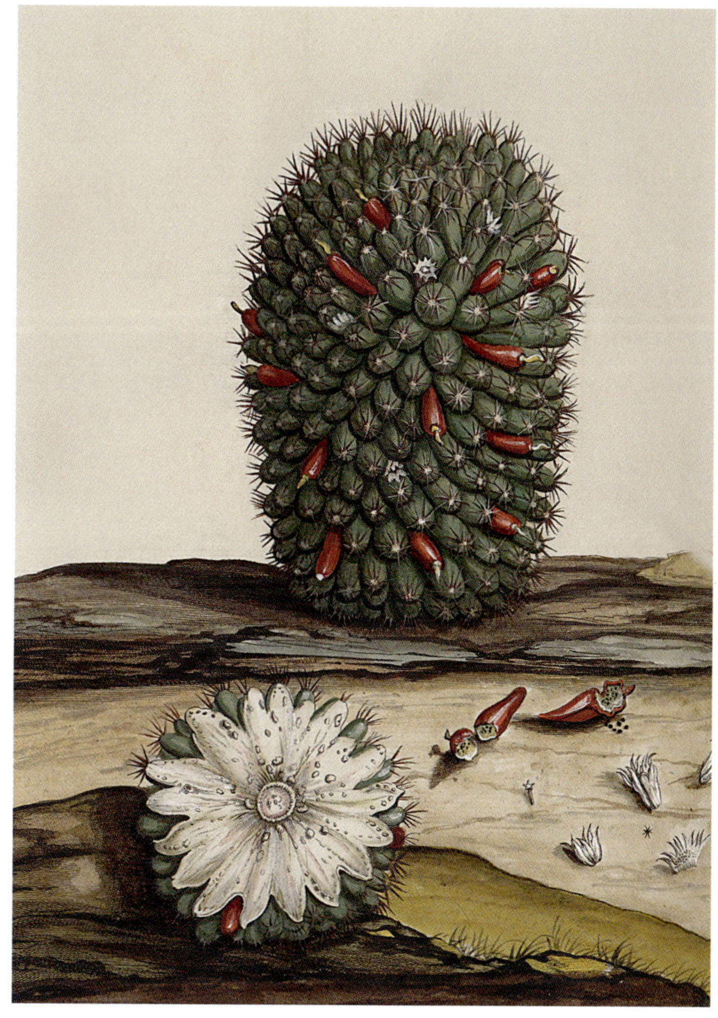

Mammillaria mammillaris

From Jan Commelin,
Horti medici Amstelodamensis,
1697

RCIN 1057108

Plums, apple, grapes,
a butterfly and blossom

Anonymous, *c.*1880

RCIN 931927

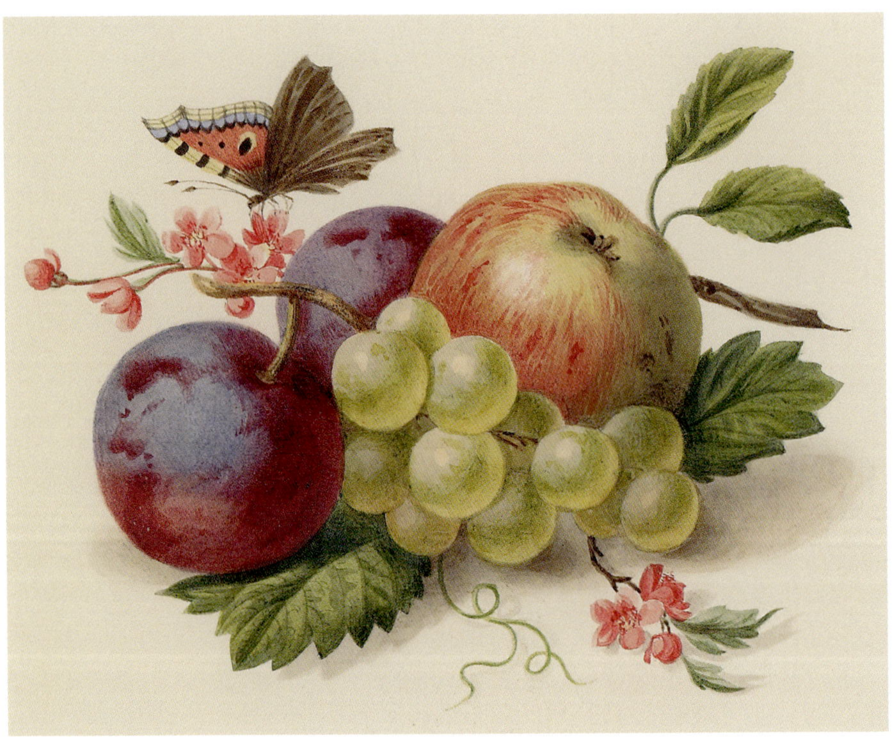

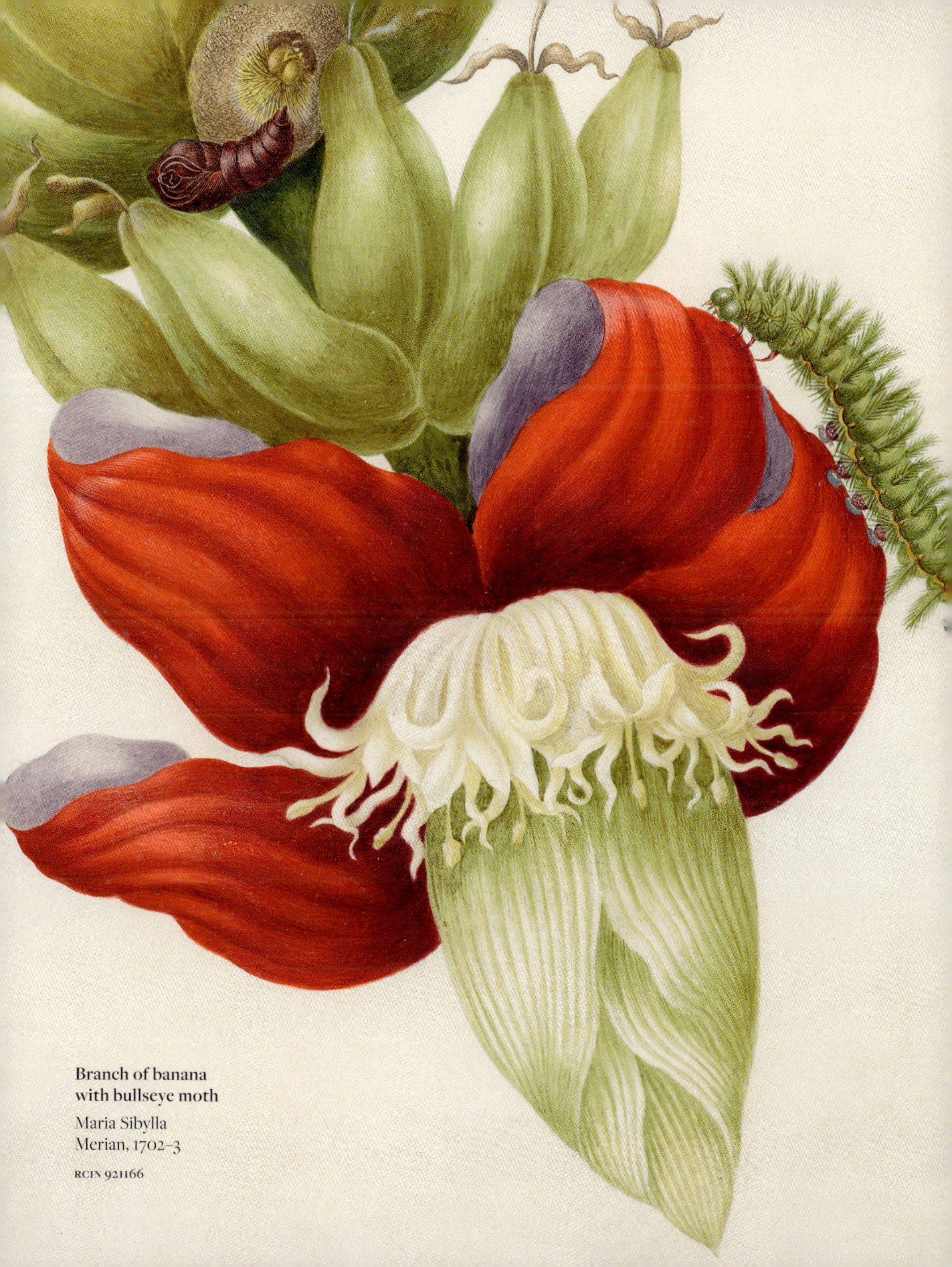

Branch of banana
with bullseye moth

Maria Sibylla
Merian, 1702–3

RCIN 921166

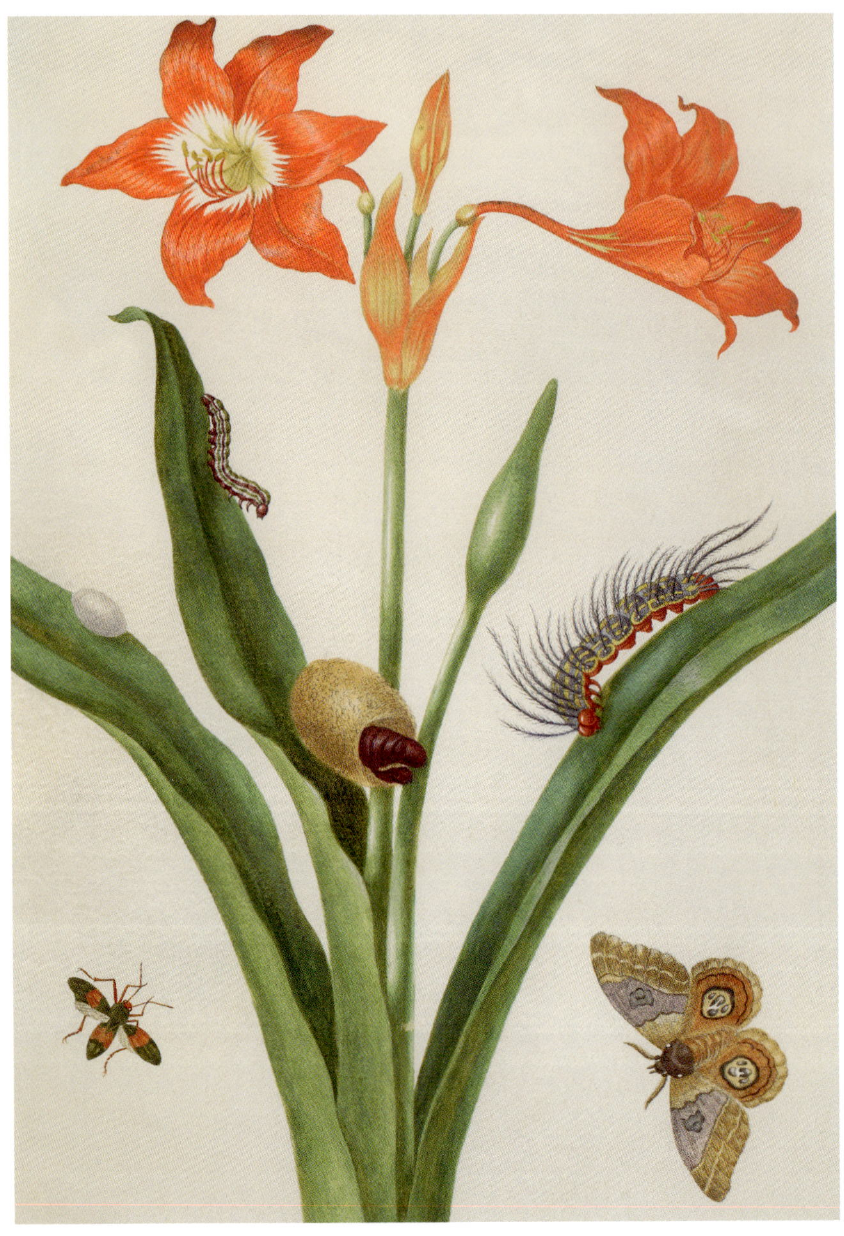

Barbados lily with bullseye moth and leaf-footed bug

Maria Sibylla Merian, 1702–3

RCIN 921177

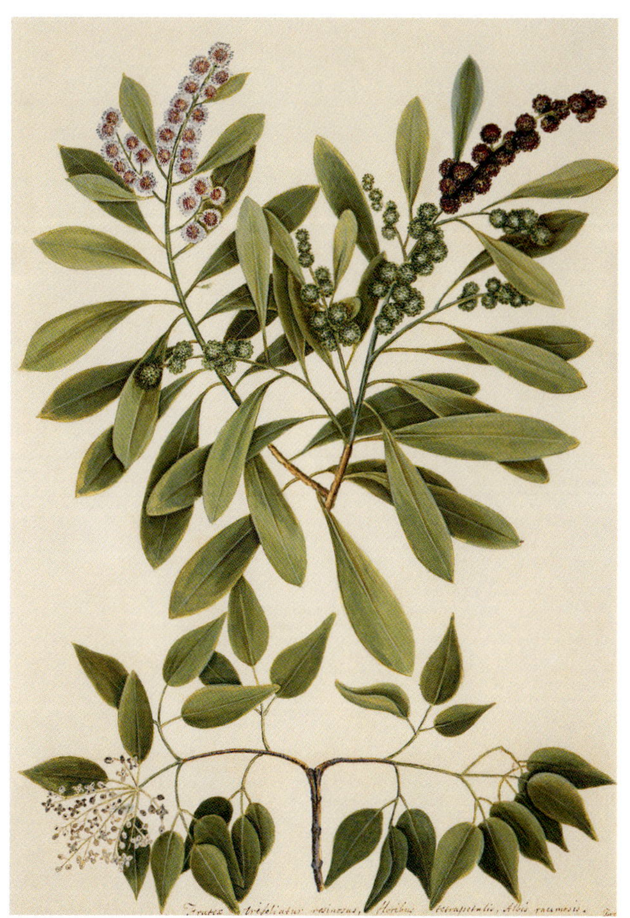

Button mangrove and sea torchwood

Mark Catesby, c.1722–6

RCIN 925979

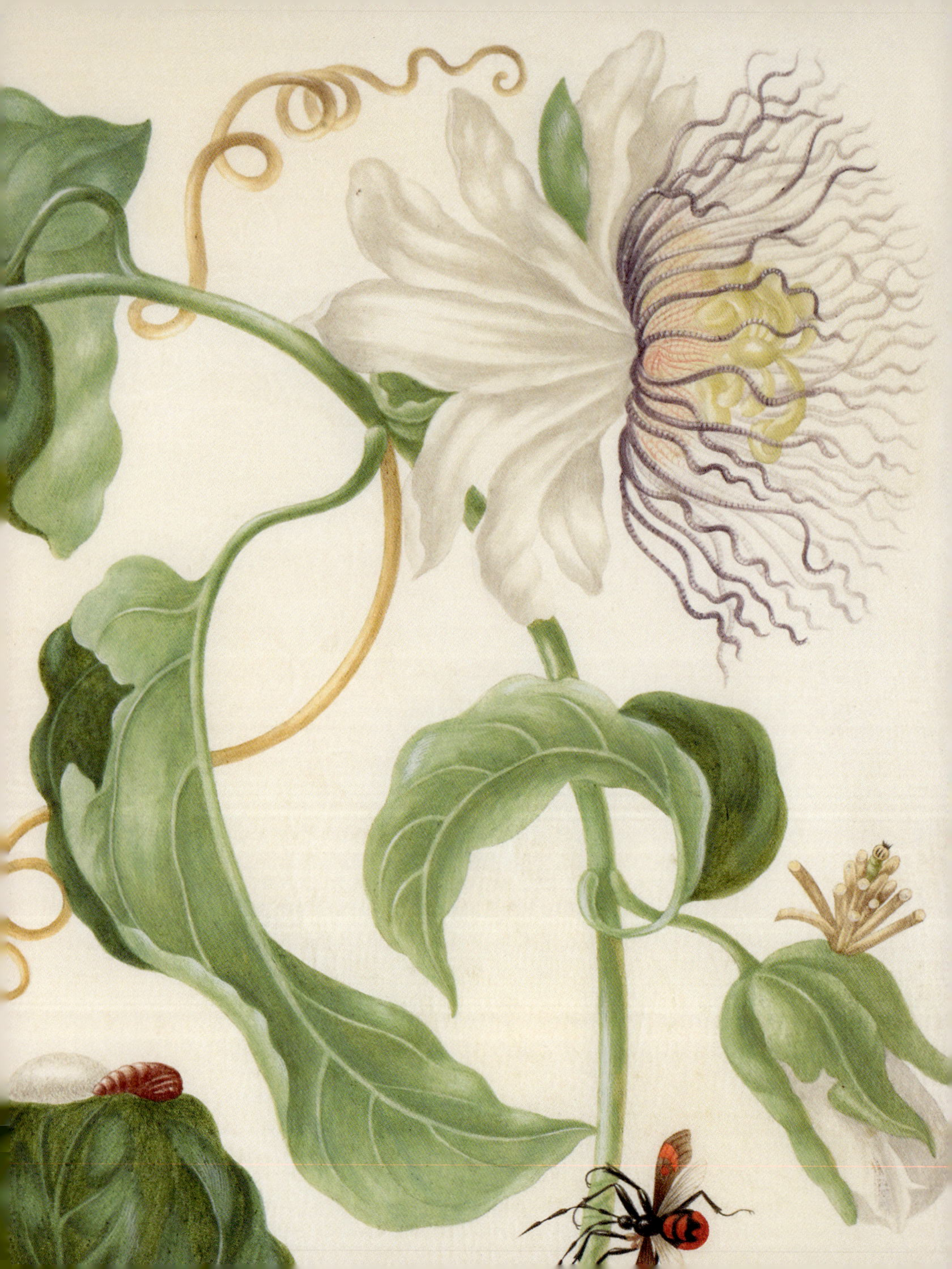

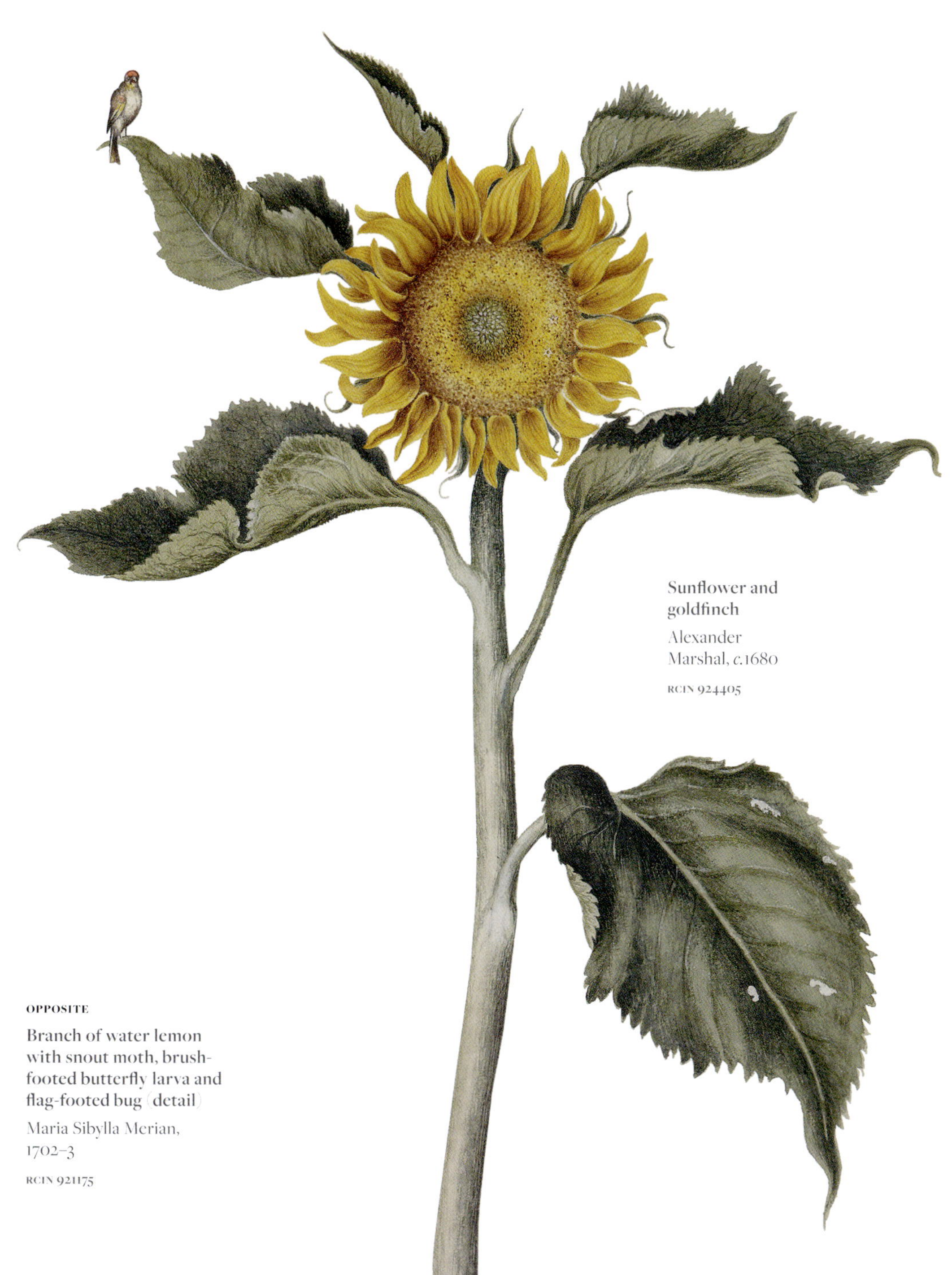

Sunflower and
goldfinch

Alexander
Marshal, *c.*1680

RCIN 924405

Branch of water lemon
with snout moth, brush-
footed butterfly larva and
flag-footed bug (detail)

Maria Sibylla Merian,
1702–3

RCIN 921175

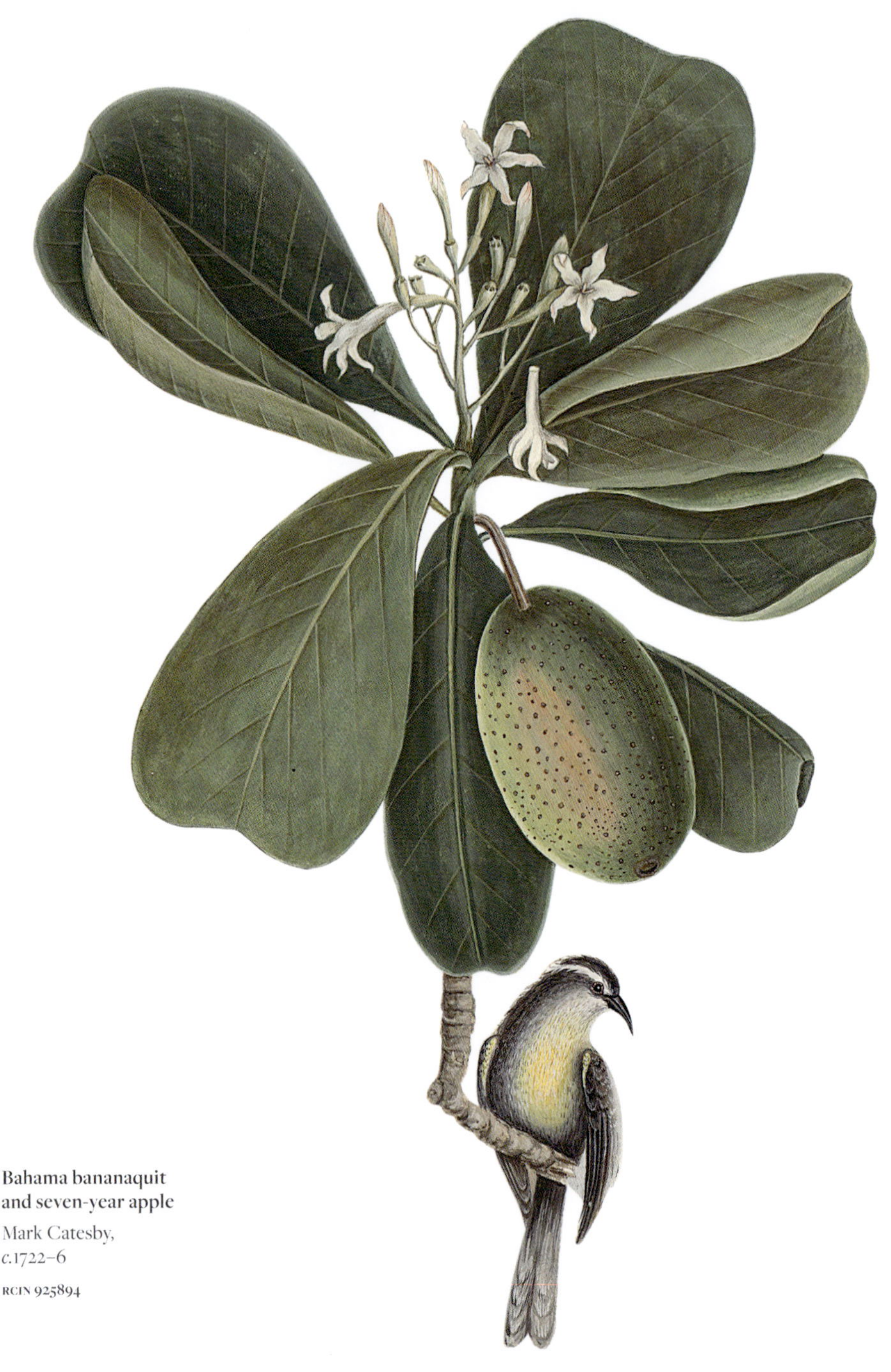

Bahama bananaquit
and seven-year apple

Mark Catesby,
*c.*1722–6

RCIN 925894

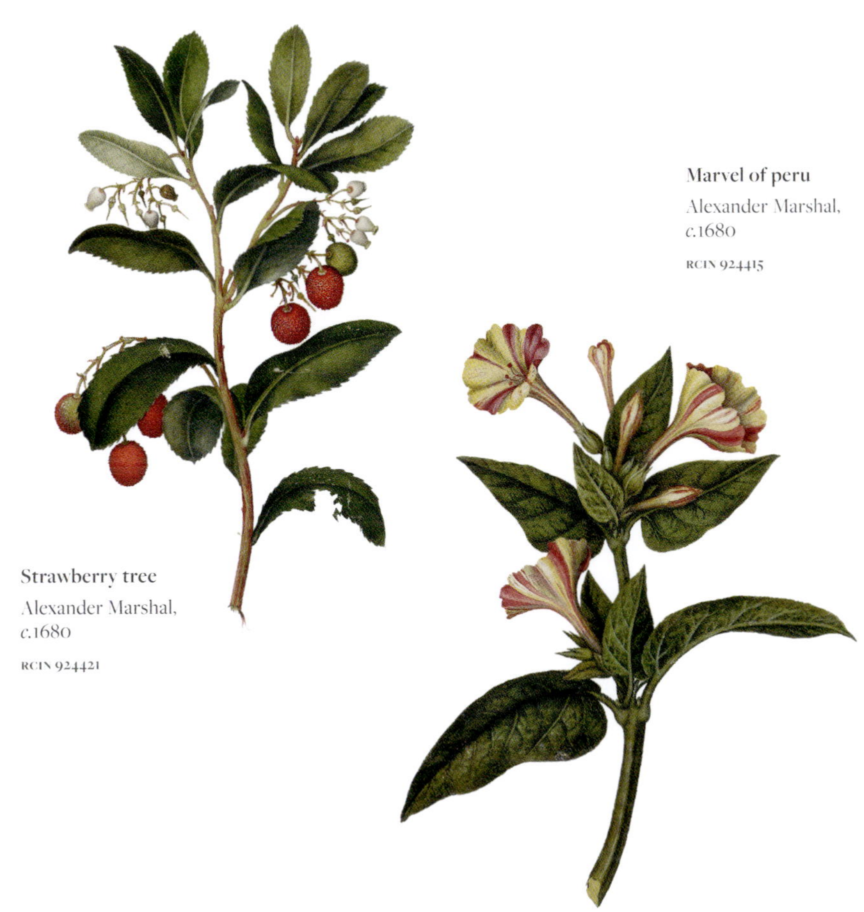

Strawberry tree

Alexander Marshal,
*c.*1680

RCIN 924421

Marvel of peru

Alexander Marshal,
*c.*1680

RCIN 924415

OVERLEAF

Umbrella tree

Mark Catesby,
*c.*1722–6

RCIN 926012

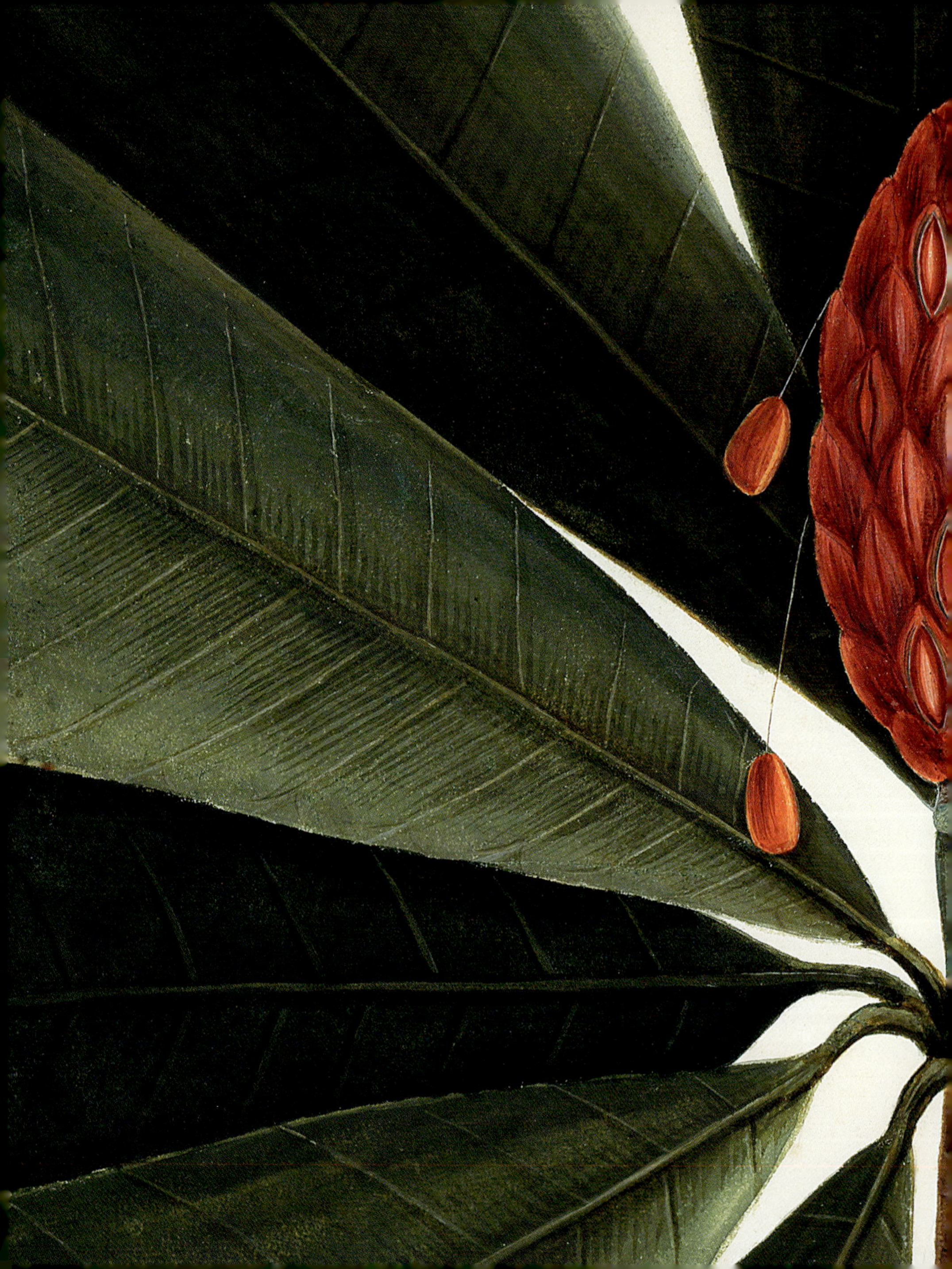

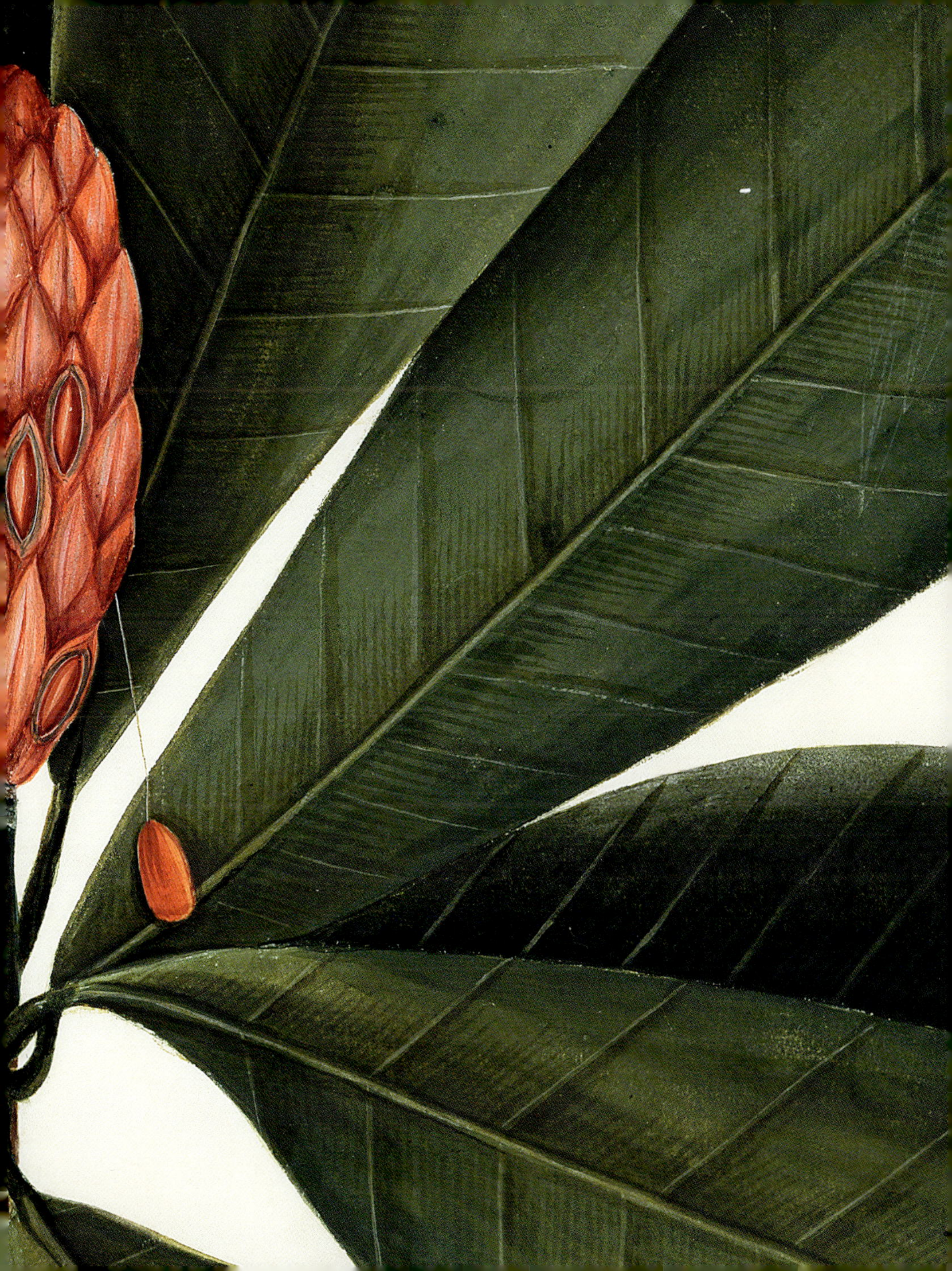

OPPOSITE

Pigeon-plum

Mark Catesby,
*c.*1722–6

RCIN 926057

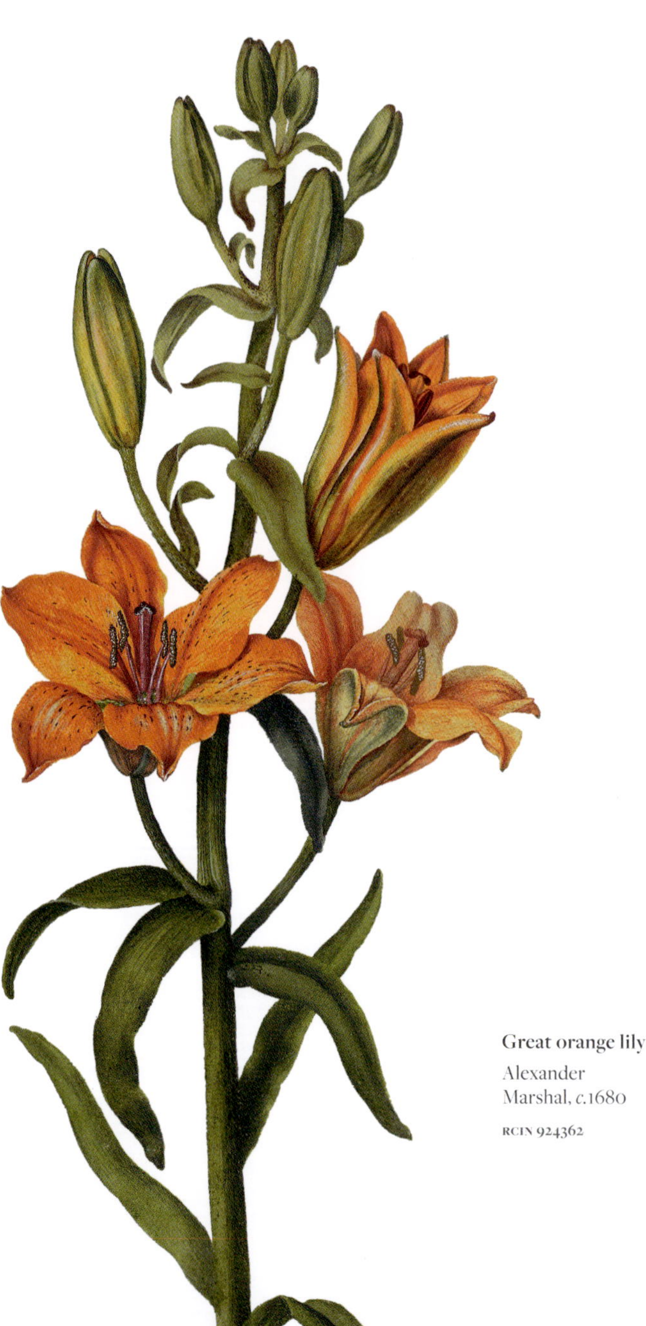

Great orange lily

Alexander
Marshal, *c.*1680

RCIN 924362

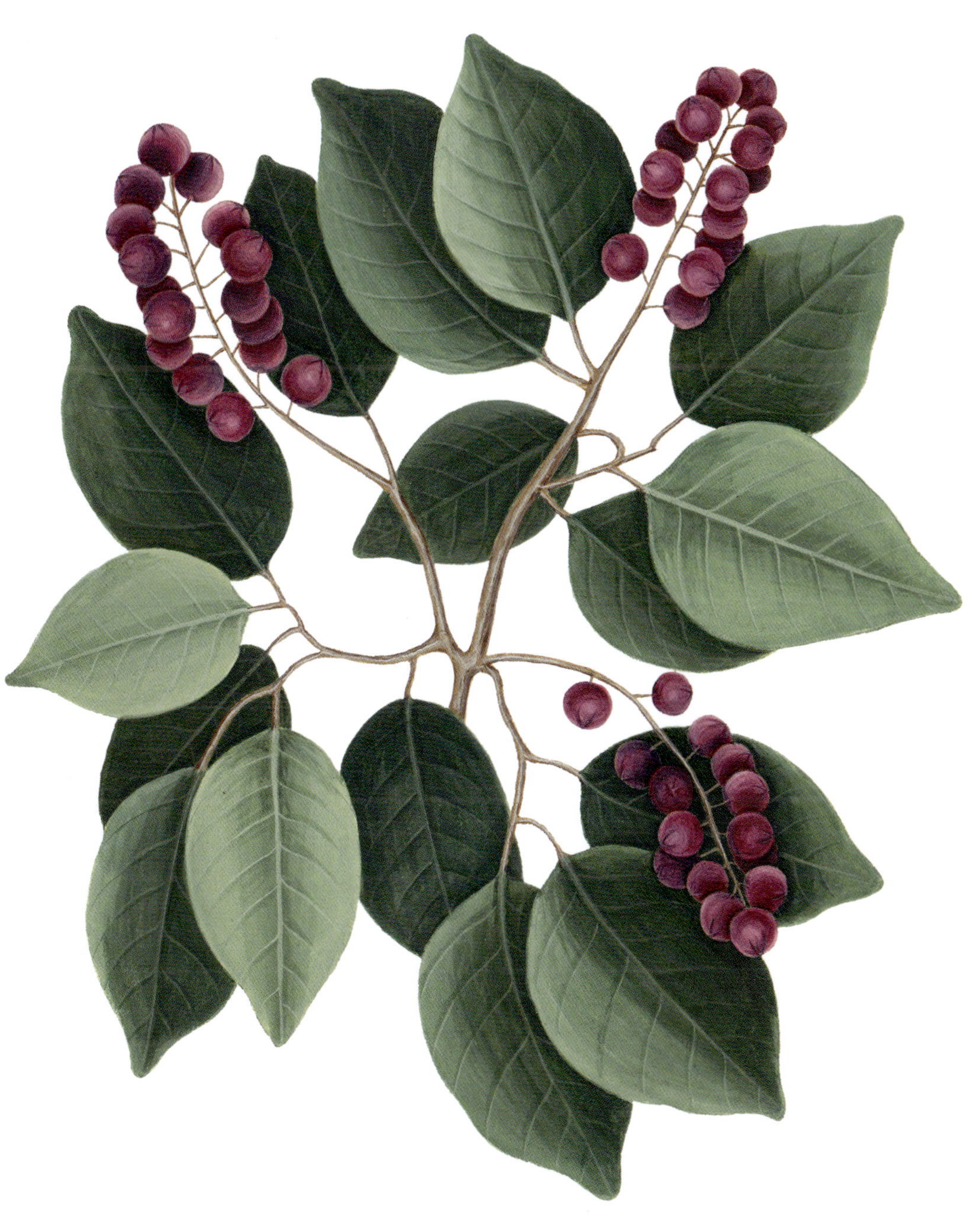

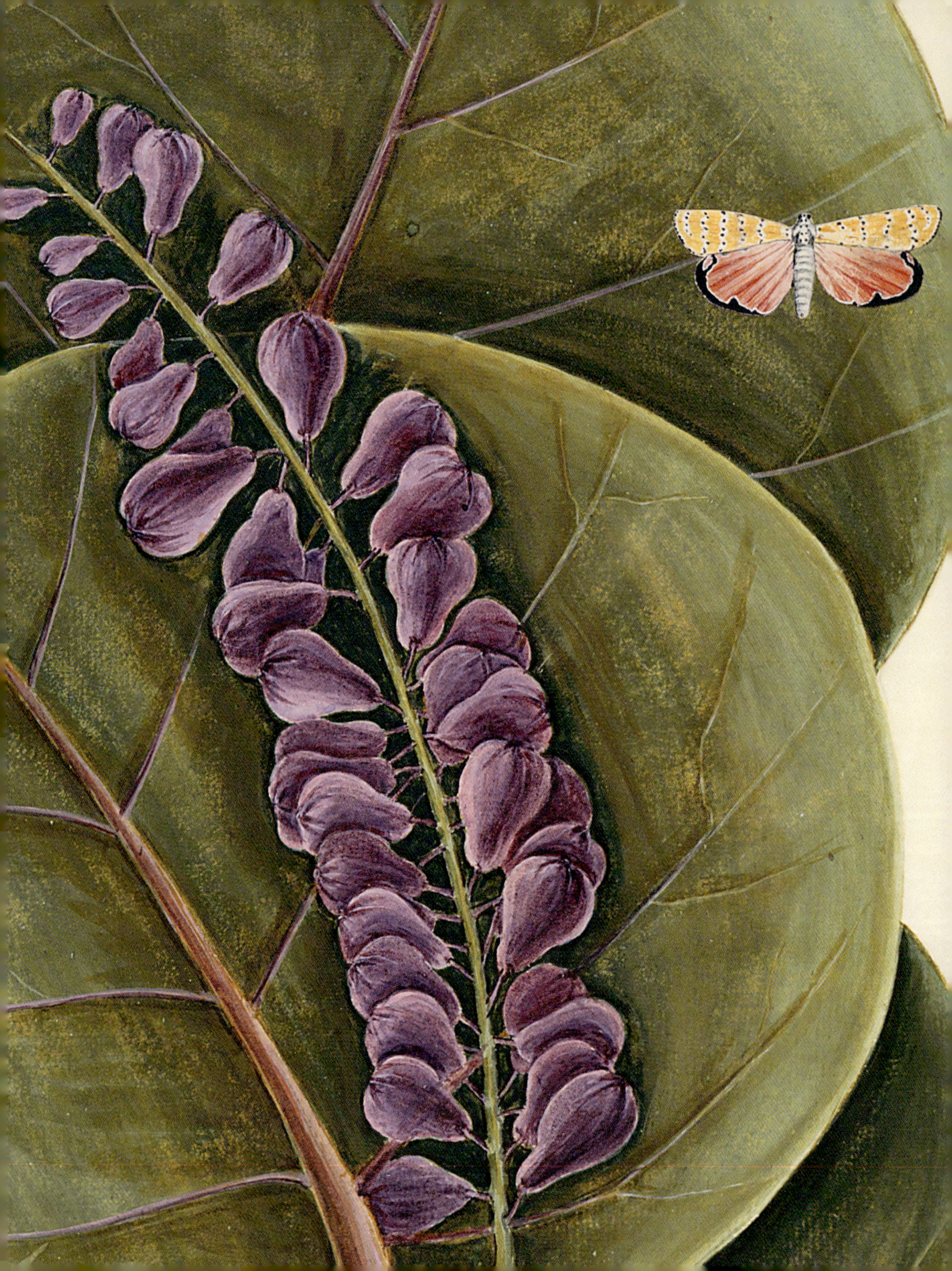

OPPOSITE

Sea-grape and
bella moth (detail)

Mark Catesby,
*c.*1722–6

RCIN 926059

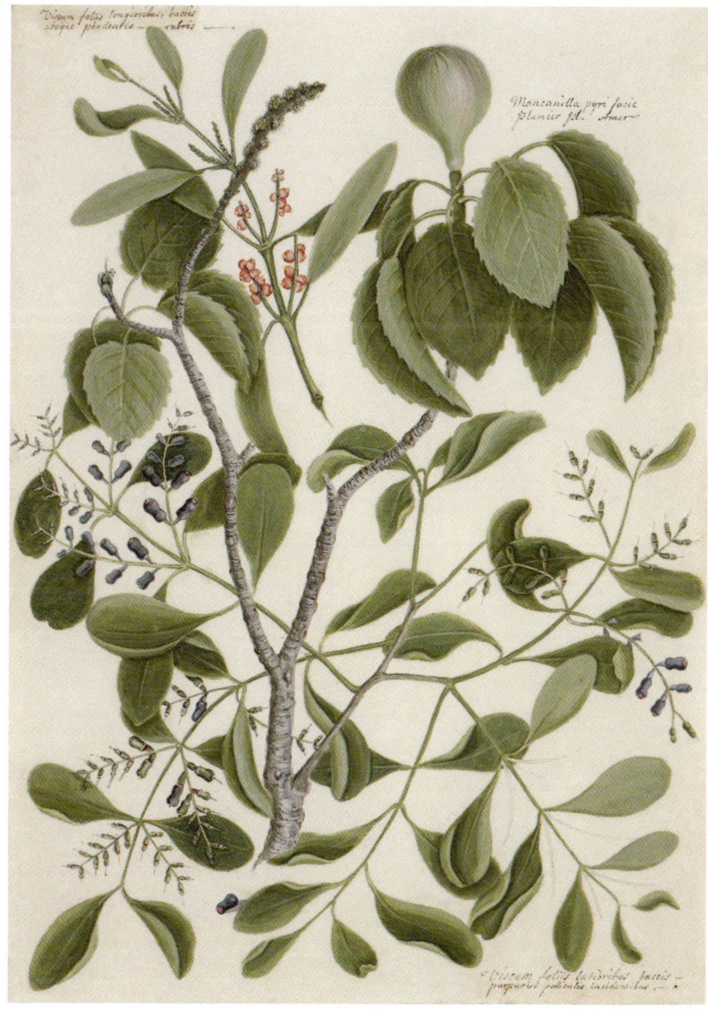

Manchineel tree,
smooth leechbush and
mahogany mistletoe

Mark Catesby, *c.*1722–6

RCIN 926058

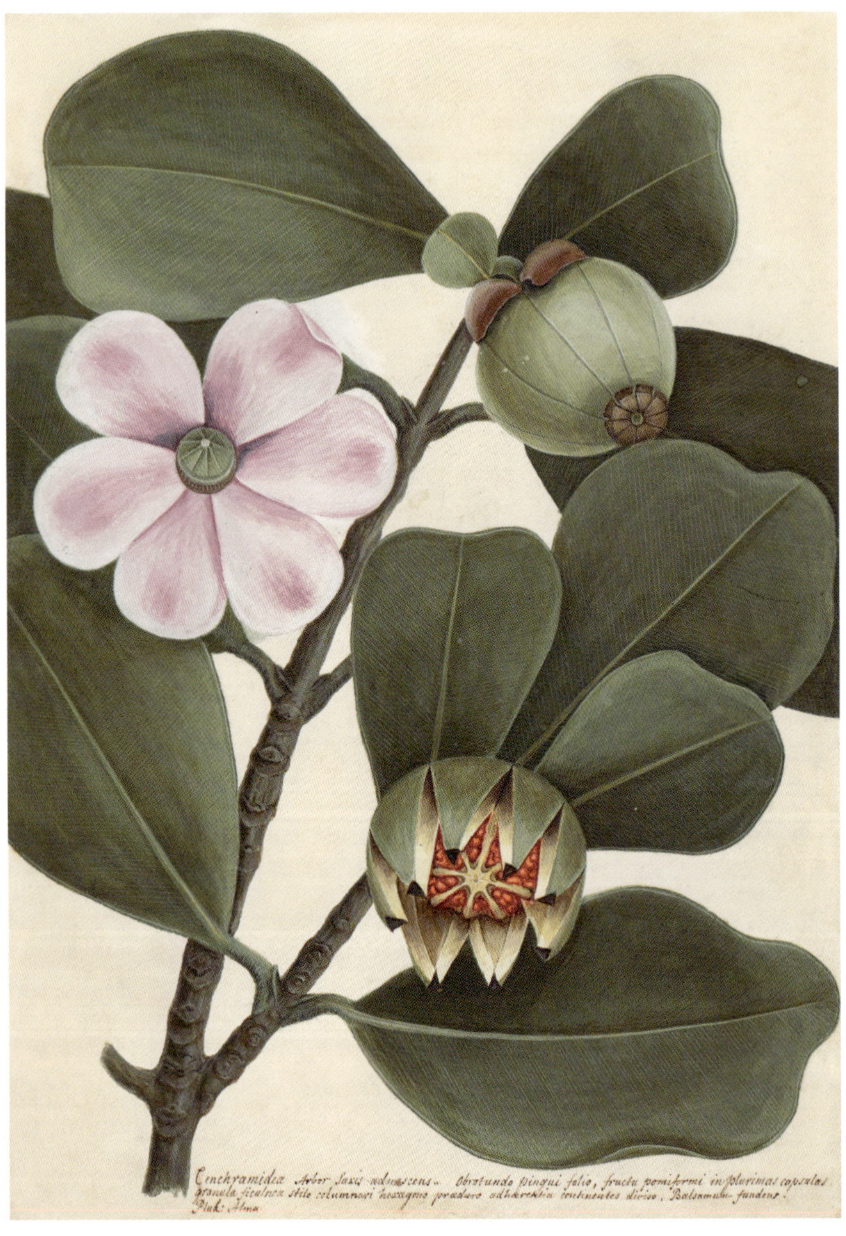

Cenchramidea Arbor Saxis adnascens. Obrotundo pingui folio, fructu pomiformi in plurimas capsulas
granula ficulnea stilo columnari hexagono praeduro adhaerentia continentes diviso. Balsamum fundens.
Pluk: Alma

Pitch apple

Mark Catesby,
*c.*1722–6

RCIN 926063

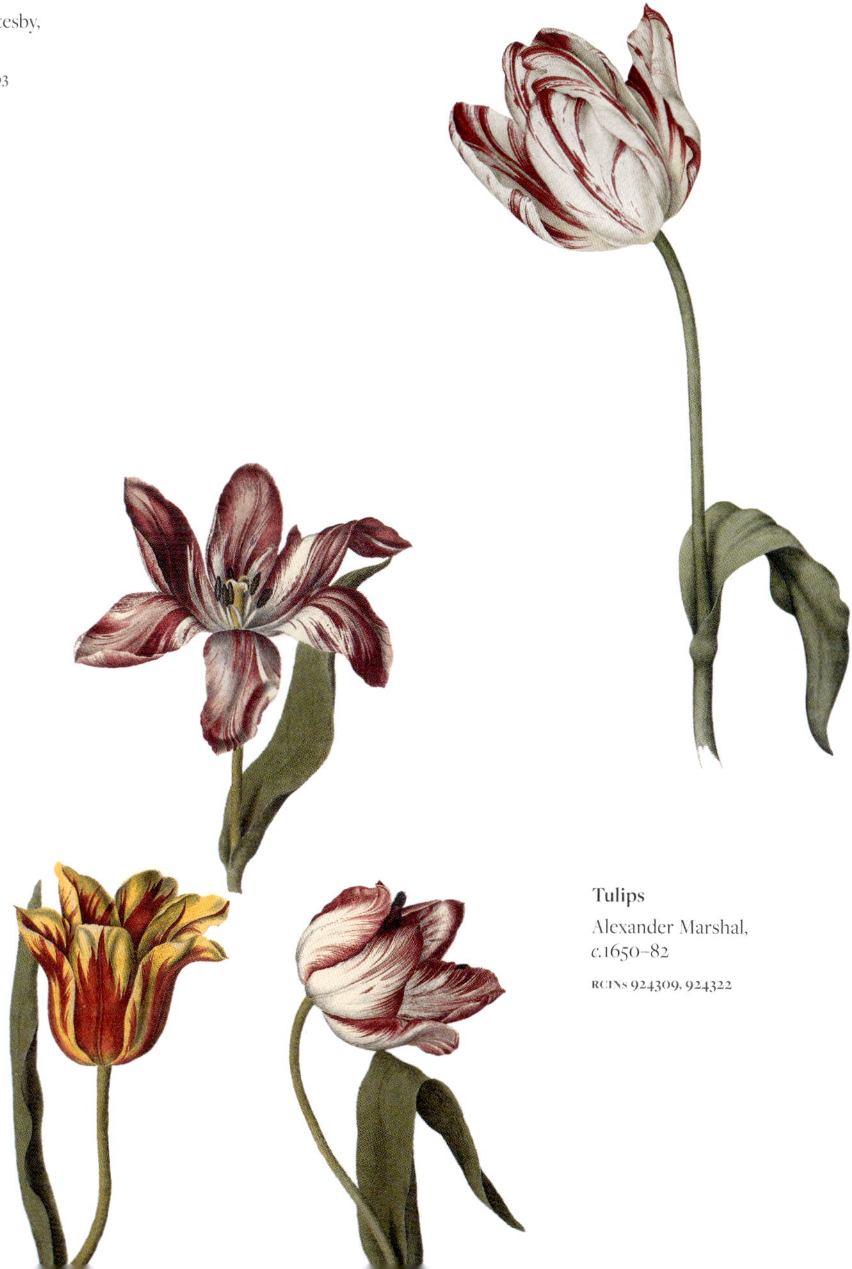

Tulips

Alexander Marshal,
*c.*1650–82

RCINs 924309, 924322

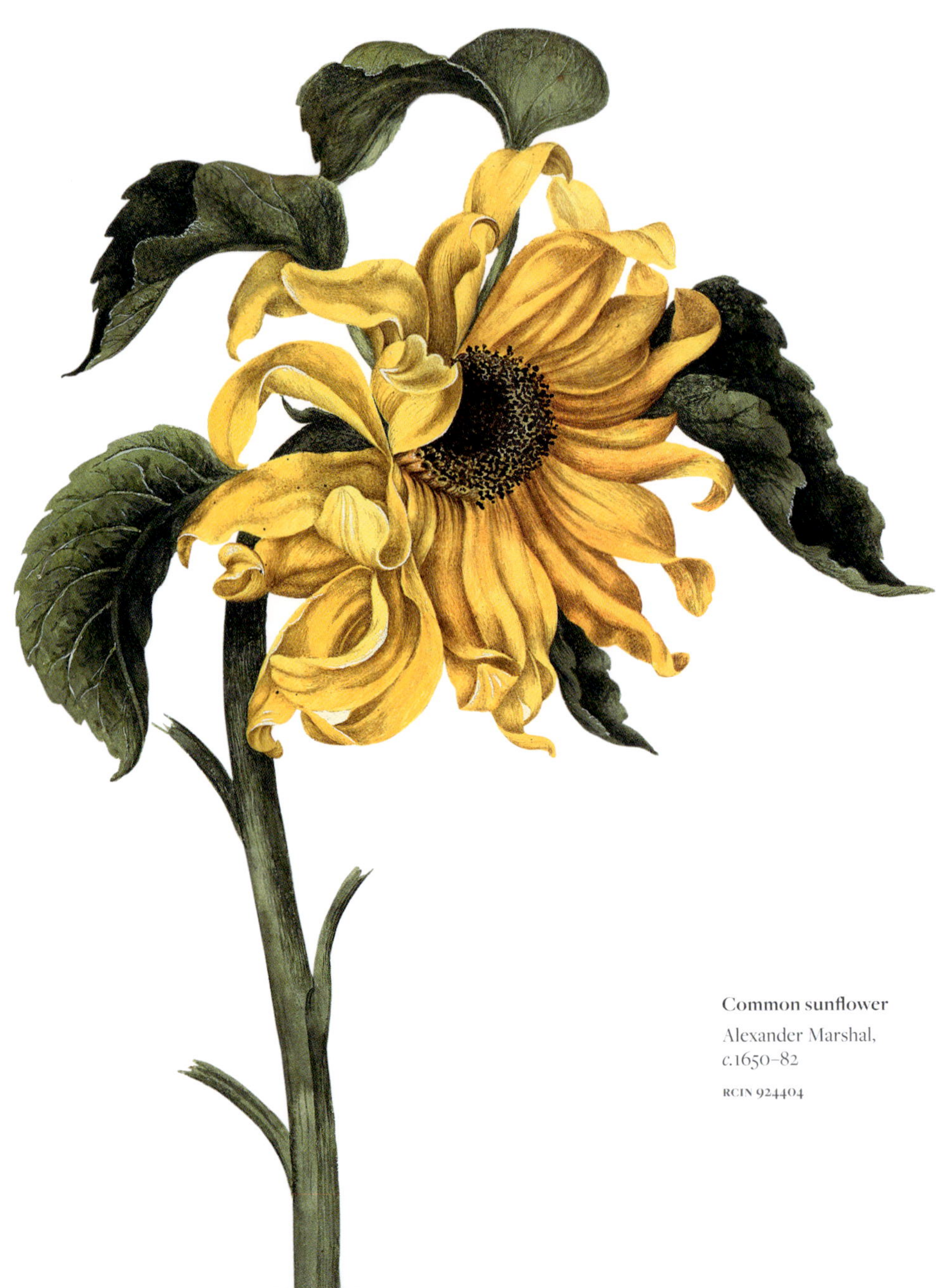

Common sunflower

Alexander Marshal,
*c.*1650–82

RCIN 924404

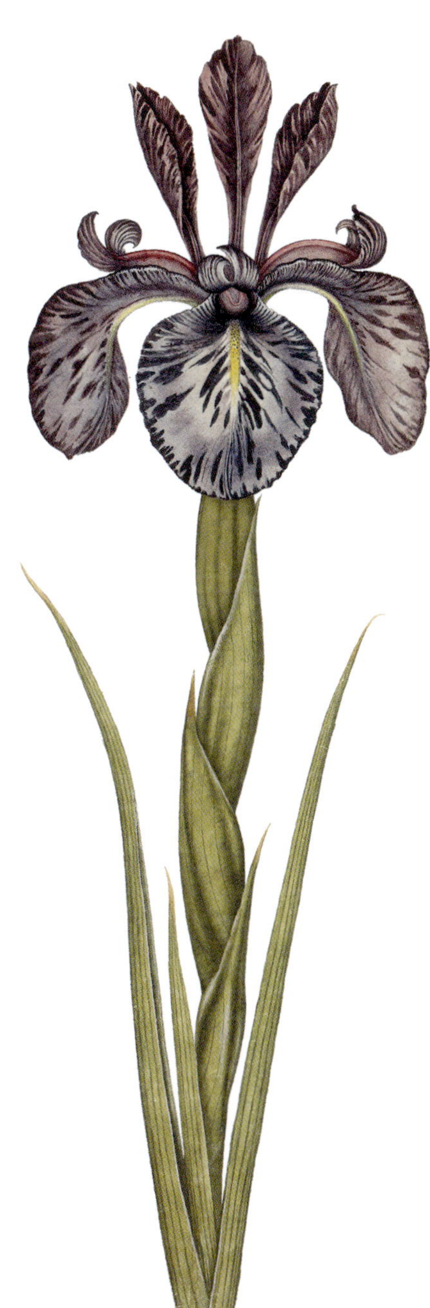

Iris (detail)
Alexander Marshal,
c.1650–82

RCIN 924337

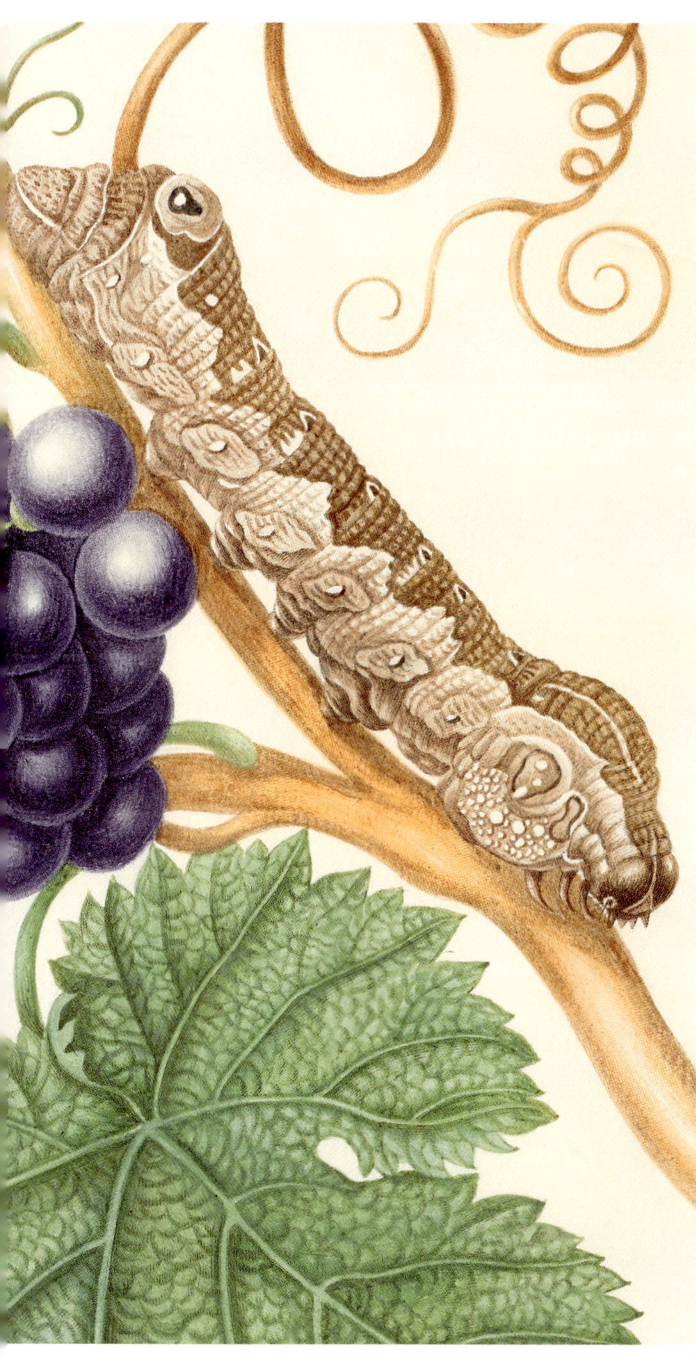

Grape vine with
gaudy sphinx moth
(detail)

Maria Sibylla Merian,
1702–3

RCIN 921190

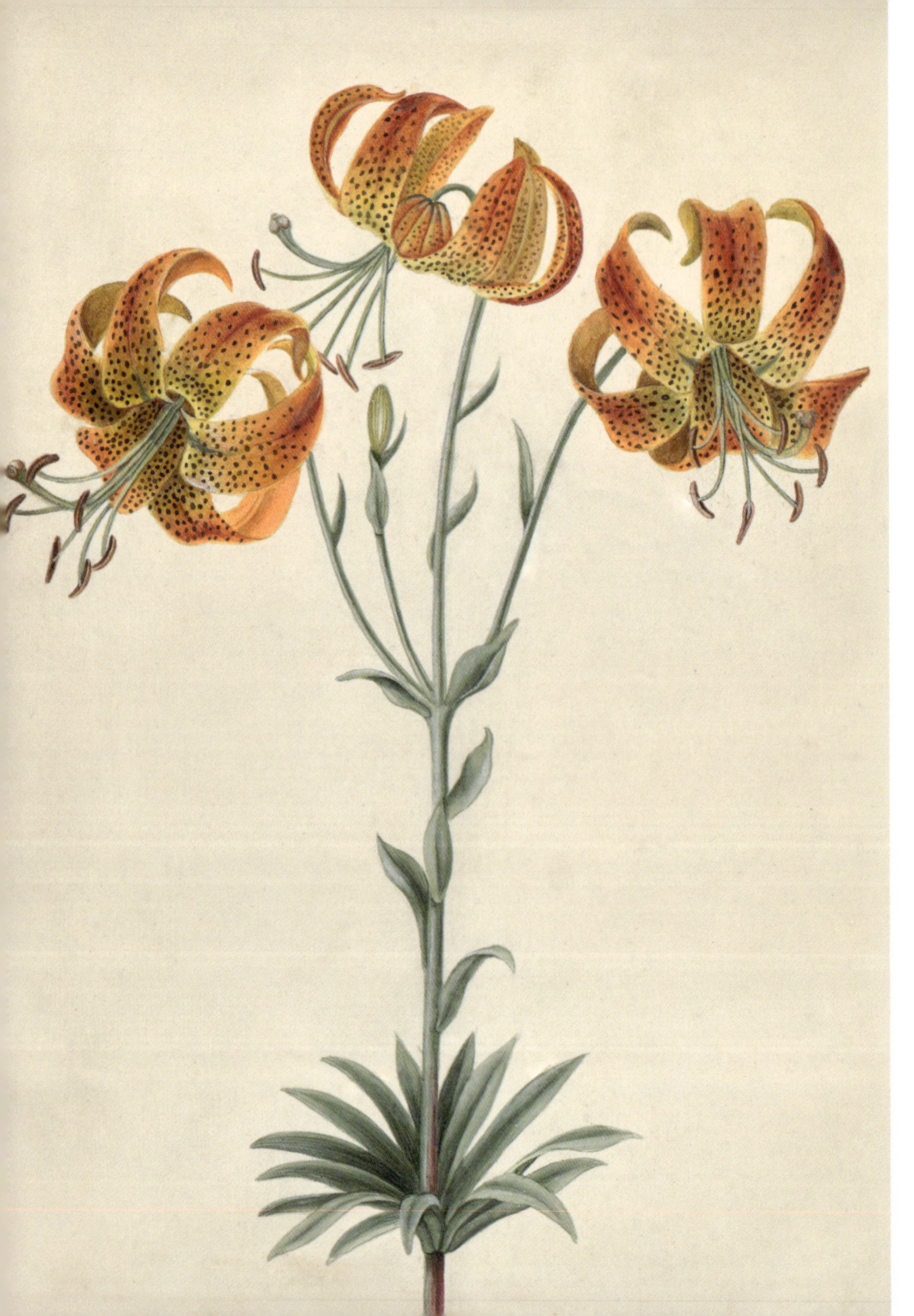

Carolina lily

Georg Dionysius
Ehret, *c*.1740

RCIN 926006

**Hollyhock
and marigold**

Alexander
Marshal, *c*.1680

RCIN 924373

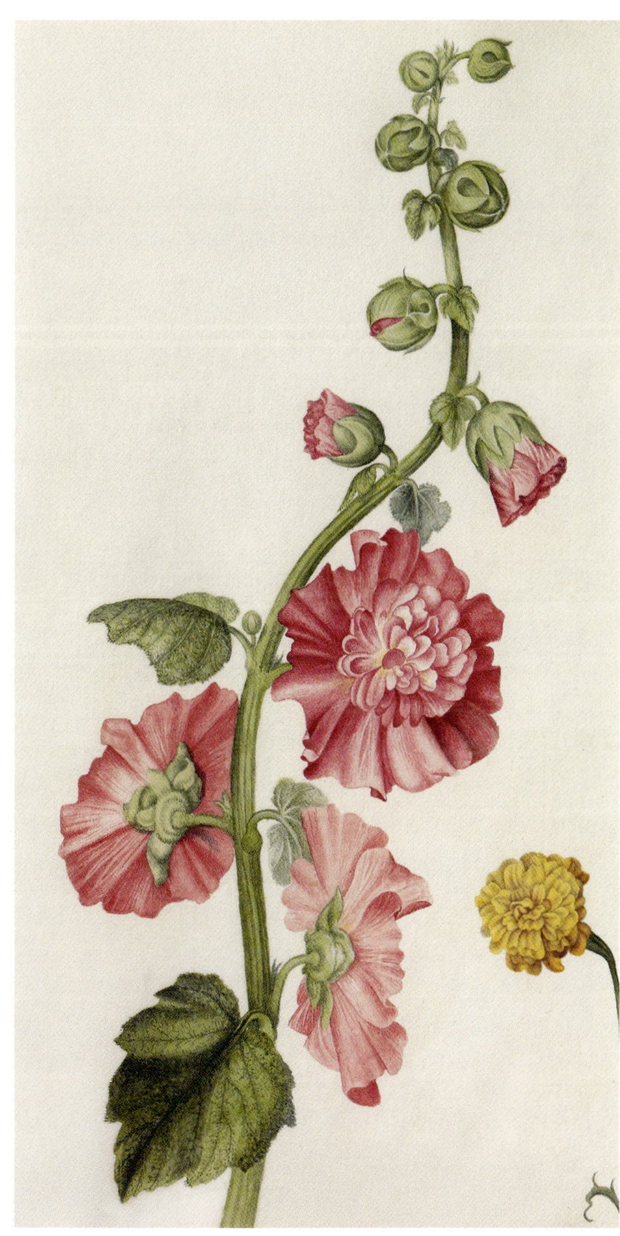

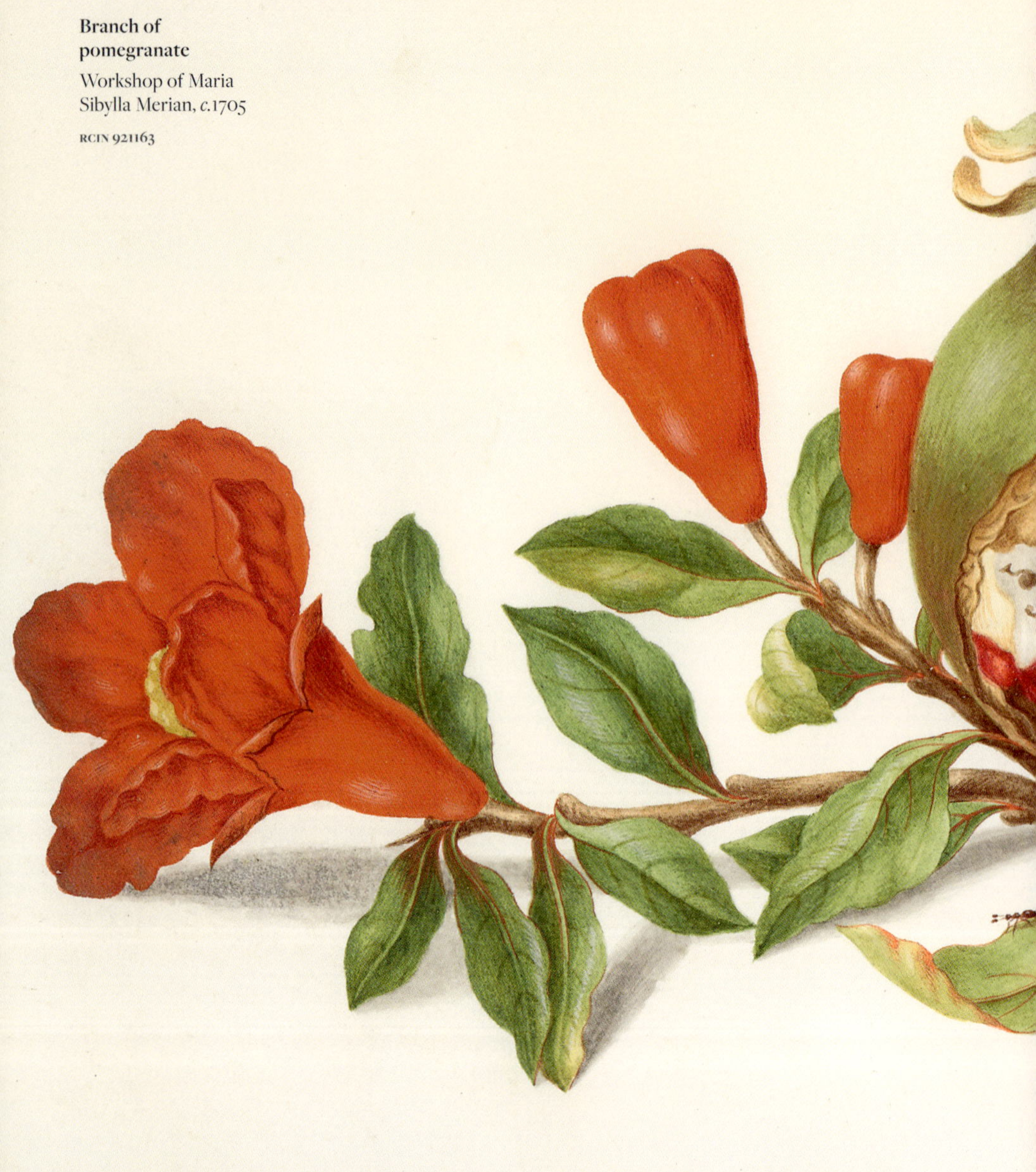

**Branch of
pomegranate**

Workshop of Maria
Sibylla Merian, *c.*1705

RCIN 921163

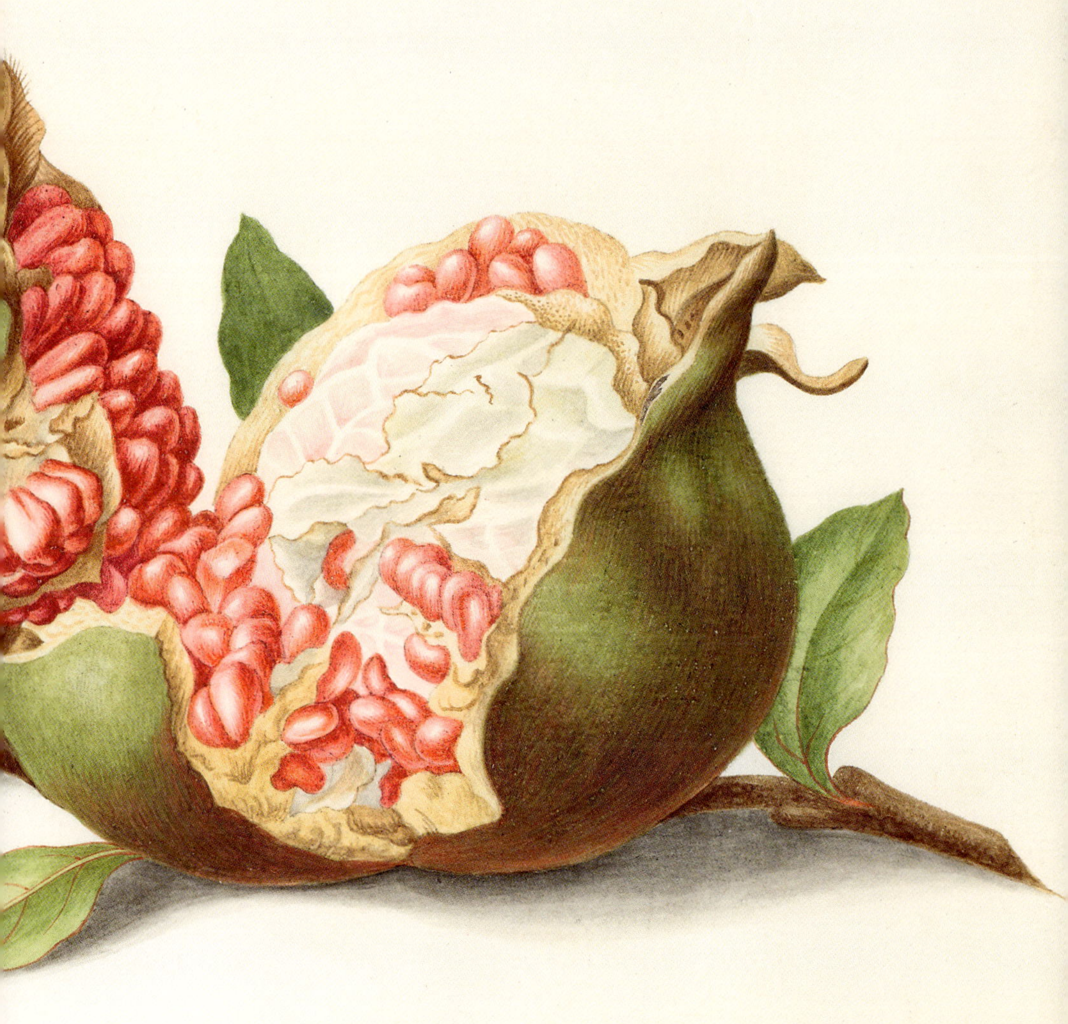

M. S. Merian. fe:

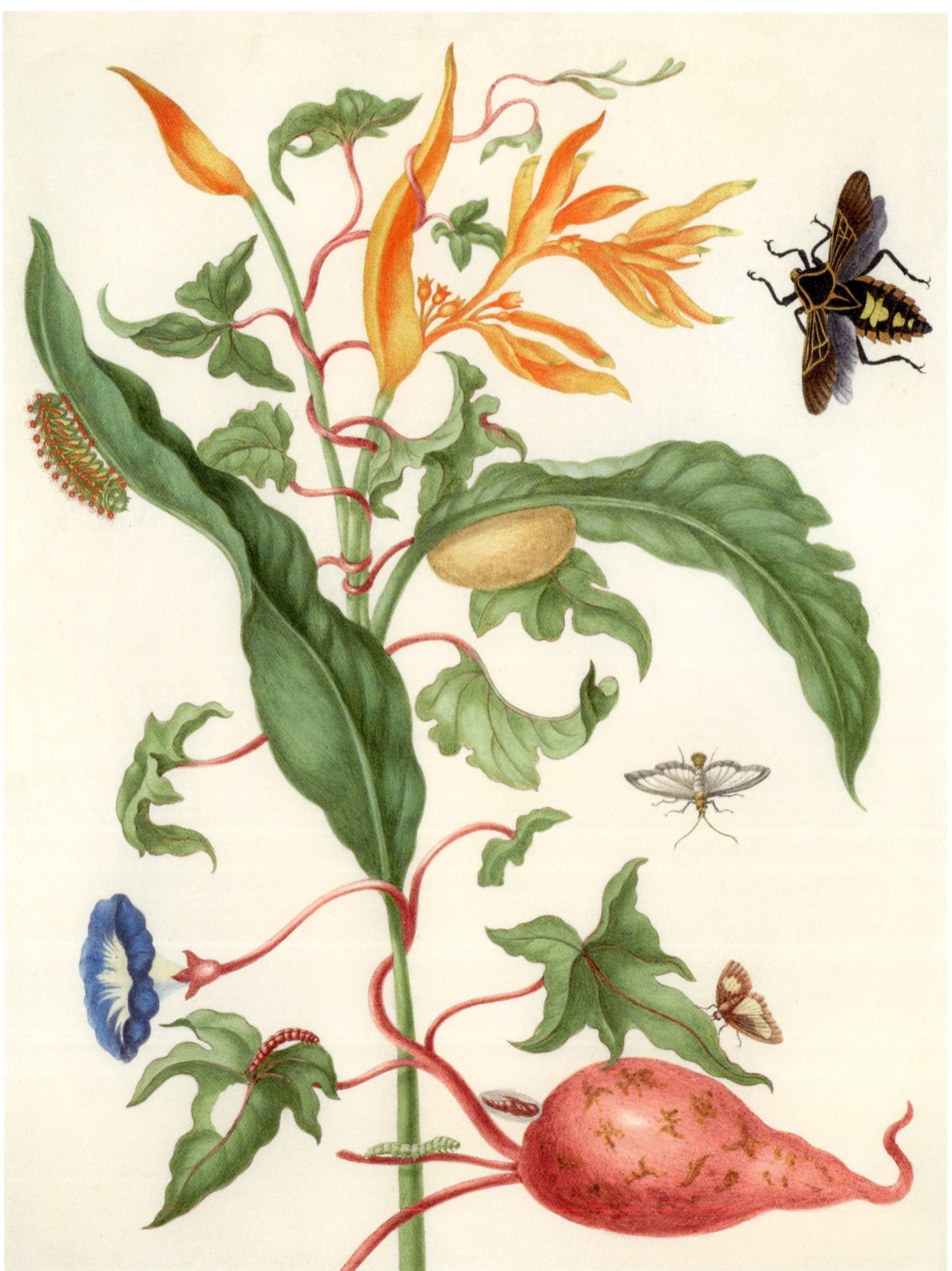

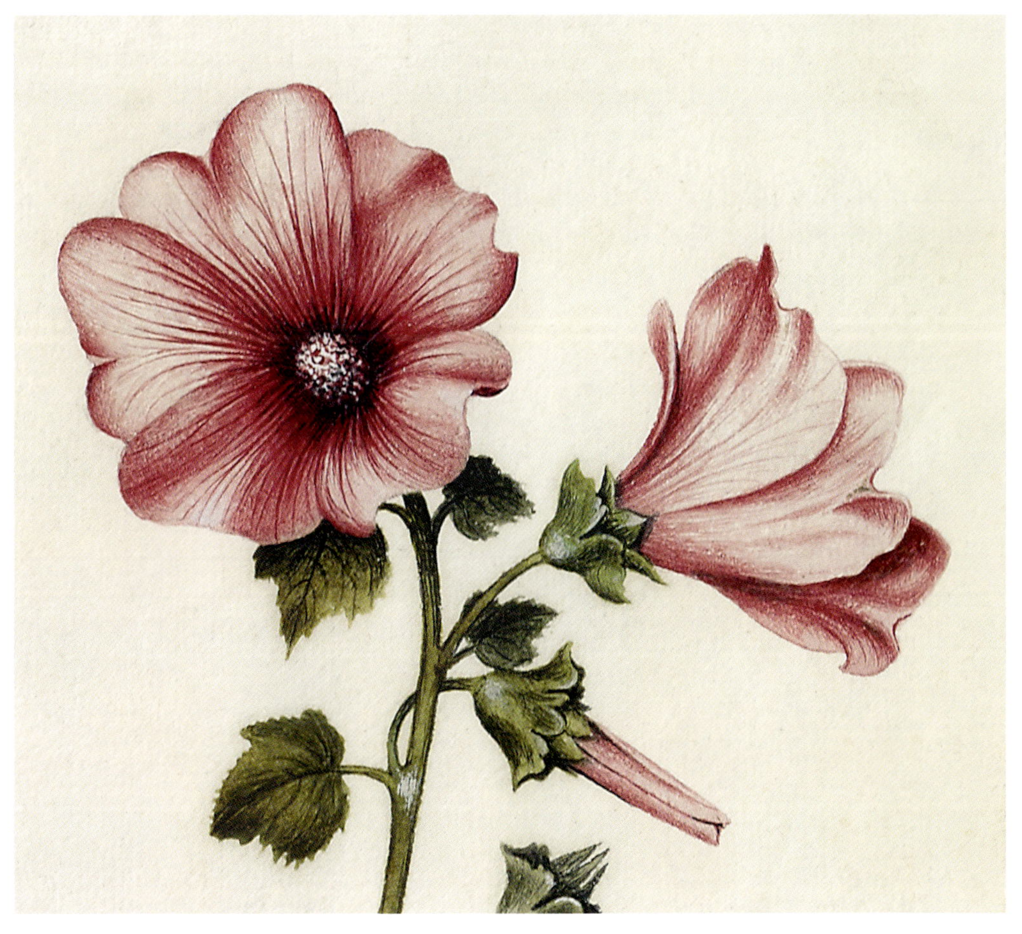

Mallow (detail)

Alexander
Marshal, *c.*1680

RCIN 924372

Sweet potato plant and
parakeet flower with a
leaf-footed bug, melonworm
moth and pickleworm moth

Maria Sibylla Merian, 1702–3

RCIN 921198

Crown imperial

Alexander Marshal,
*c.*1650–82

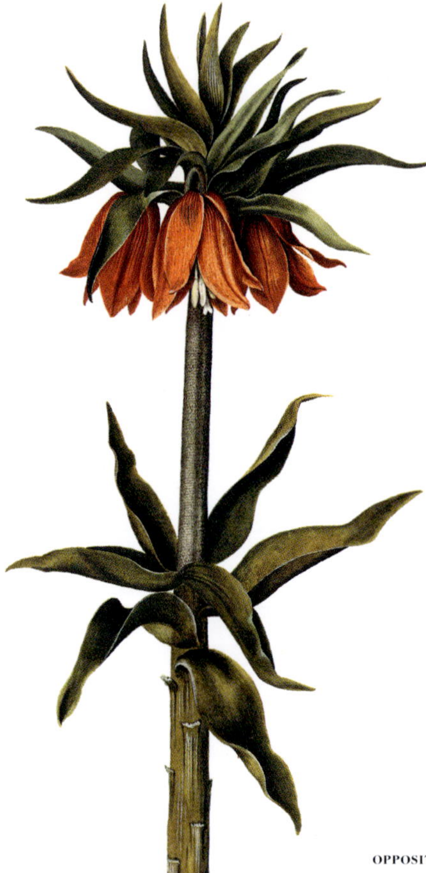

Larkspur

Alexander Marshal,
*c.*1650–82

OPPOSITE

Auriculas

From Robert John
Thornton, *Temple
of Flora*, 1807

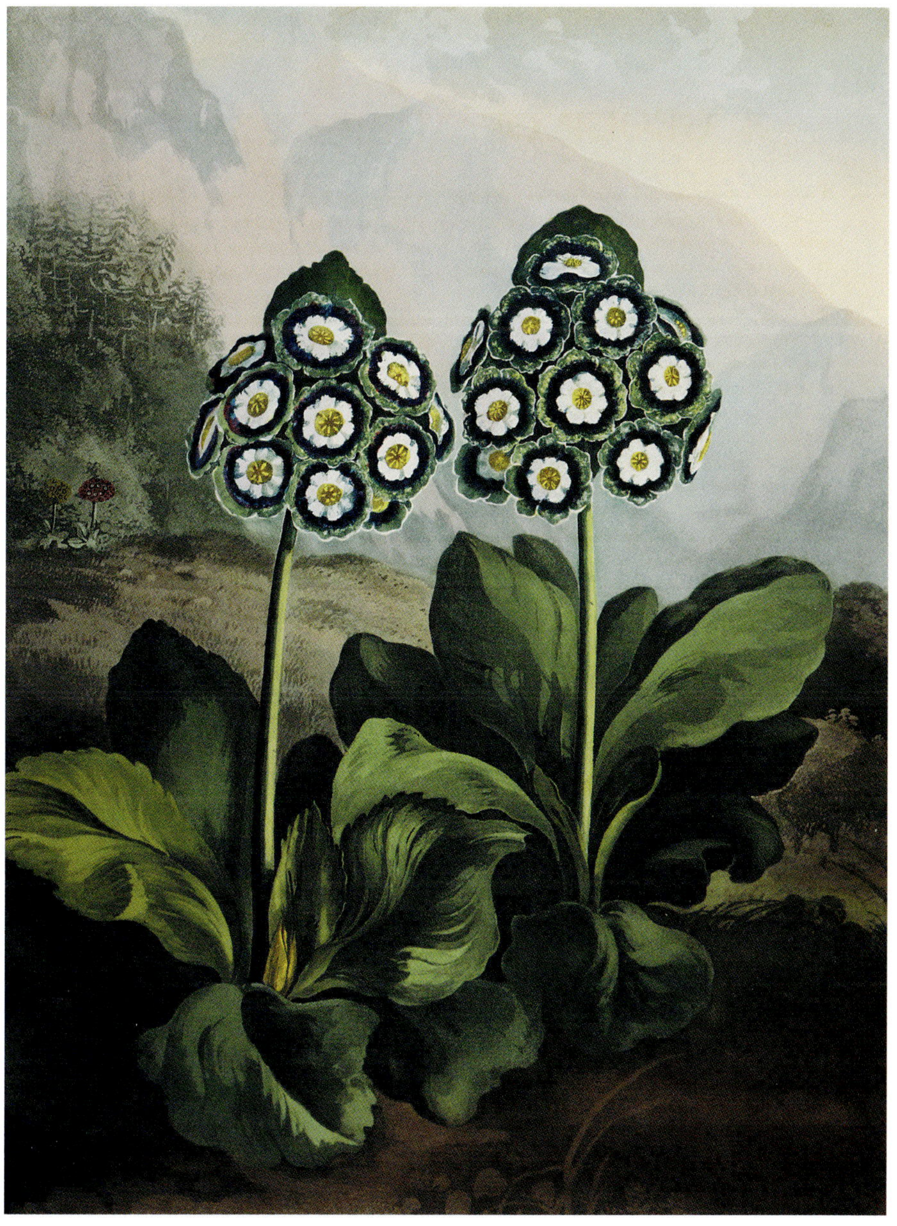

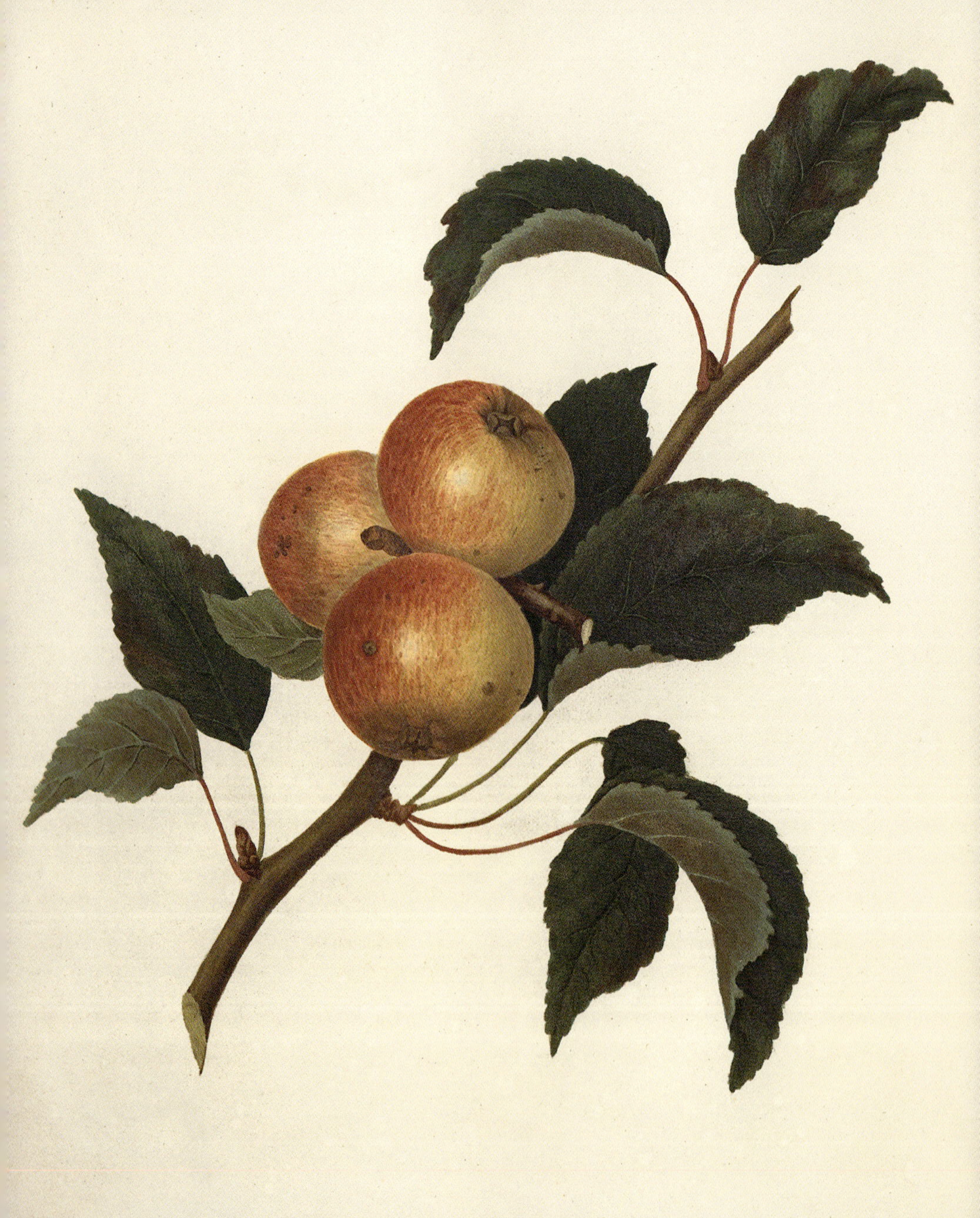

Siberian harvey

From Thomas Knight, *Pomona Herefordiensis*, 1811

RCIN 1052131

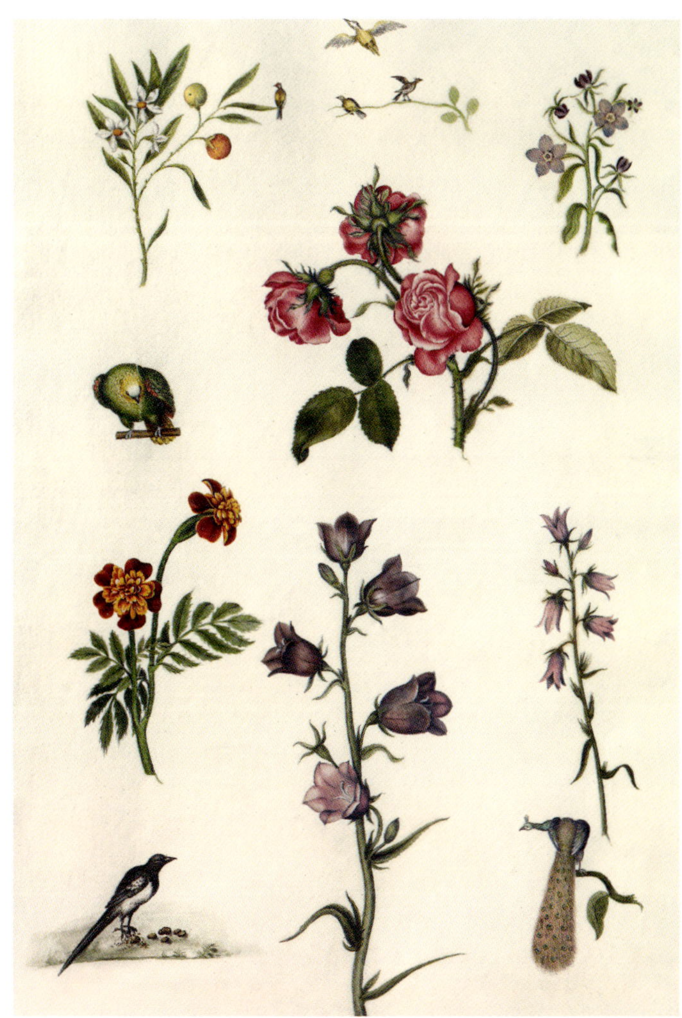

Rose, marigold, campanula bell flower, rampion and birds

Alexander Marshal, *c.*1680

RCIN 924356

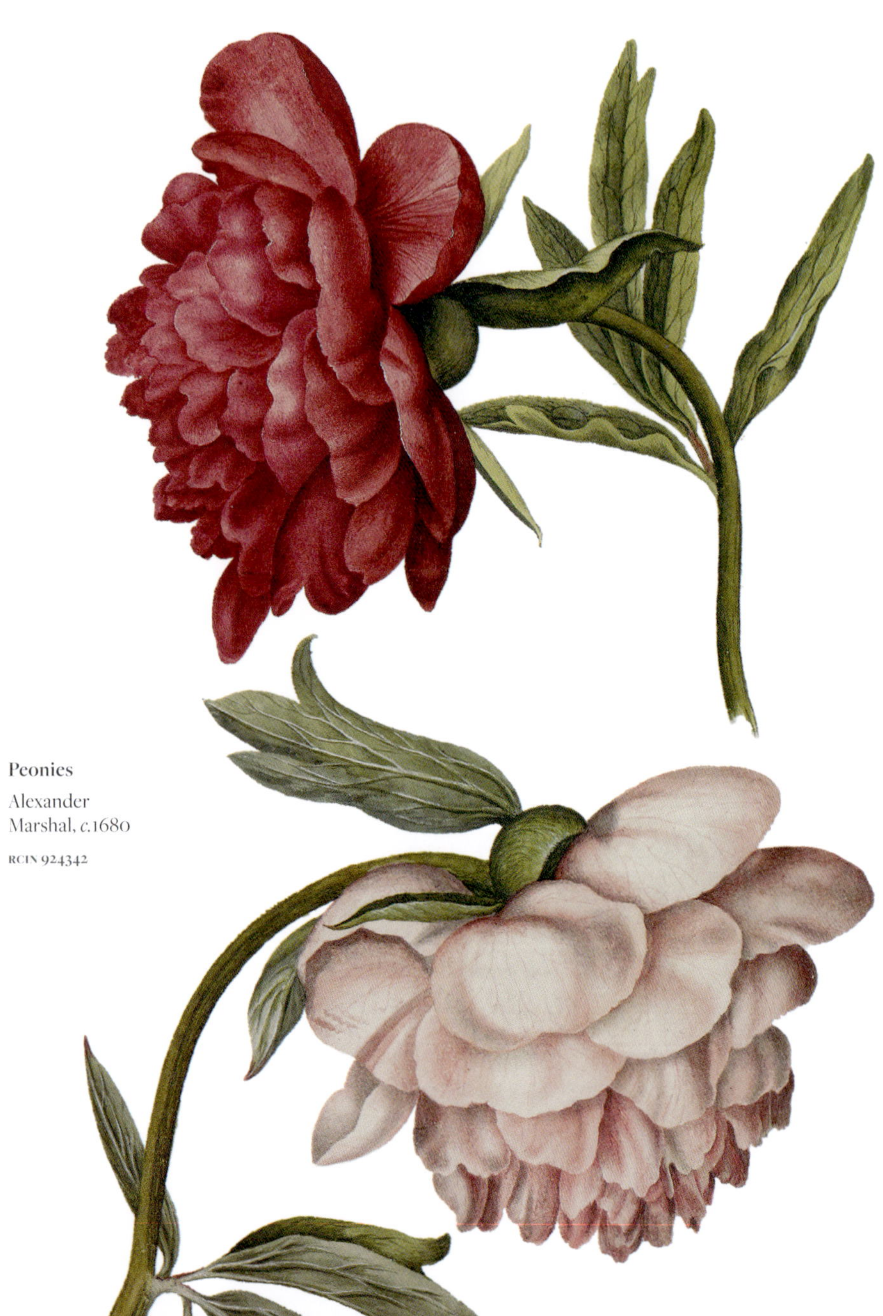

Peonies

Alexander
Marshal, *c.*1680

RCIN 924342

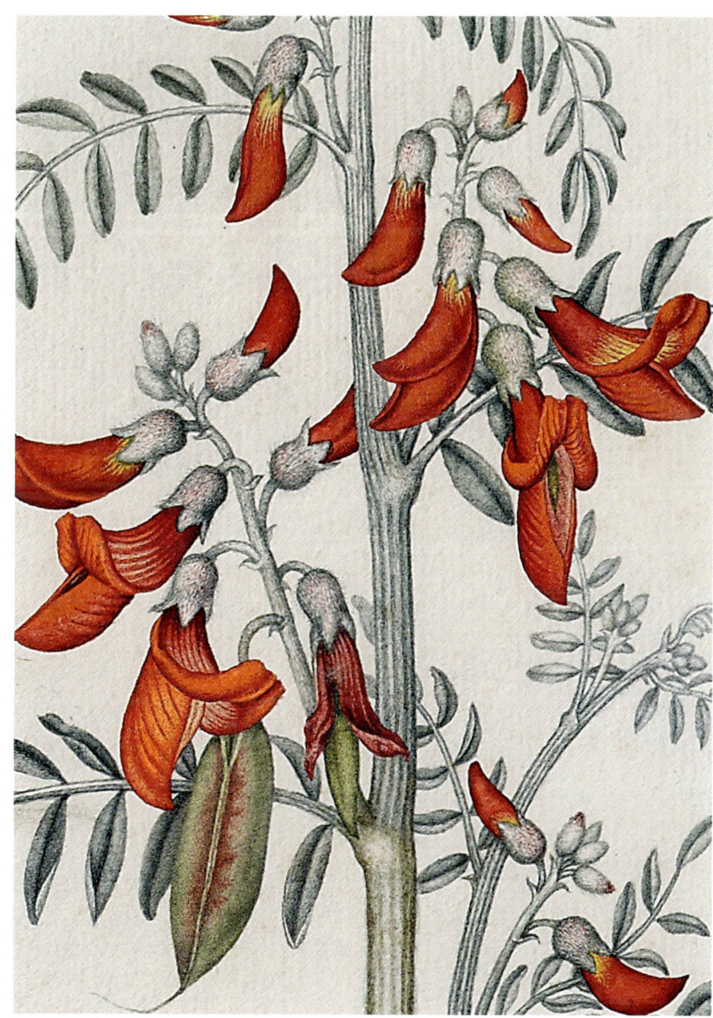

Scarlet coluthea
(detail)

Alexander
Marshal, *c.*1680

RCIN 924411

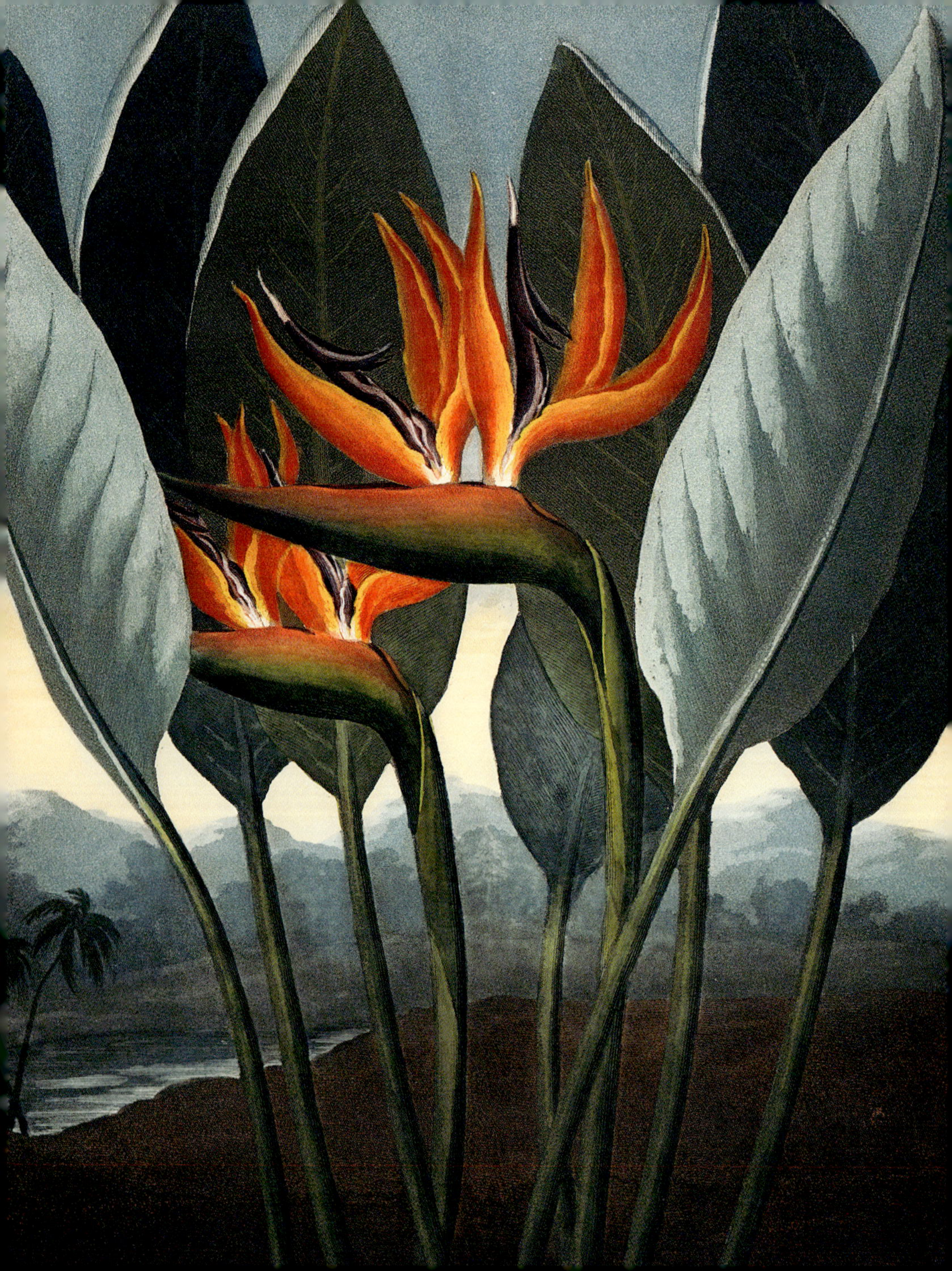

Bird of paradise flower

From Robert John Thornton, *Temple of Flora*, 1807

RCIN 1059578

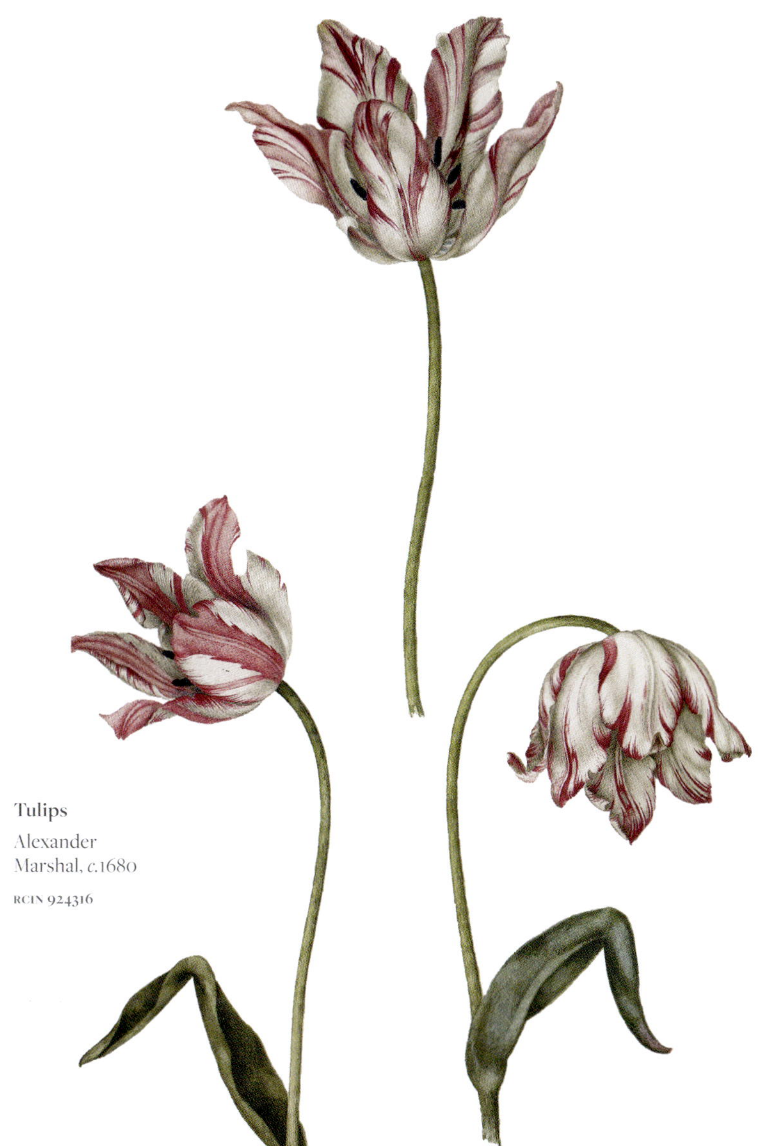

Tulips

Alexander Marshal, *c.*1680

RCIN 924316

OPPOSITE

**Papaya plant
with nymphidium
butterfly**

Maria Sibylla
Merian, 1702–3

RCIN 921197

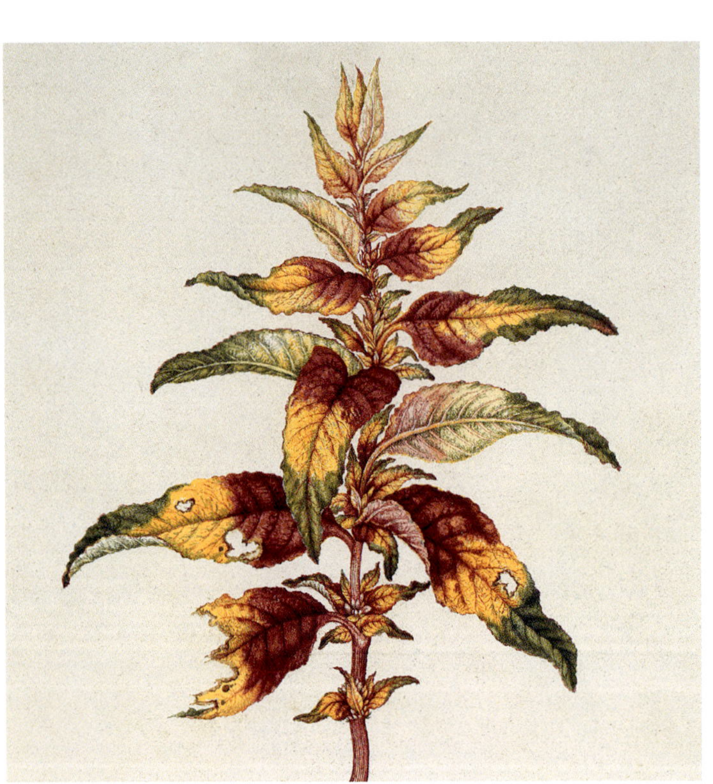

Amaranthus

Alexander Marshal,
*c.*1650–82

RCIN 924417

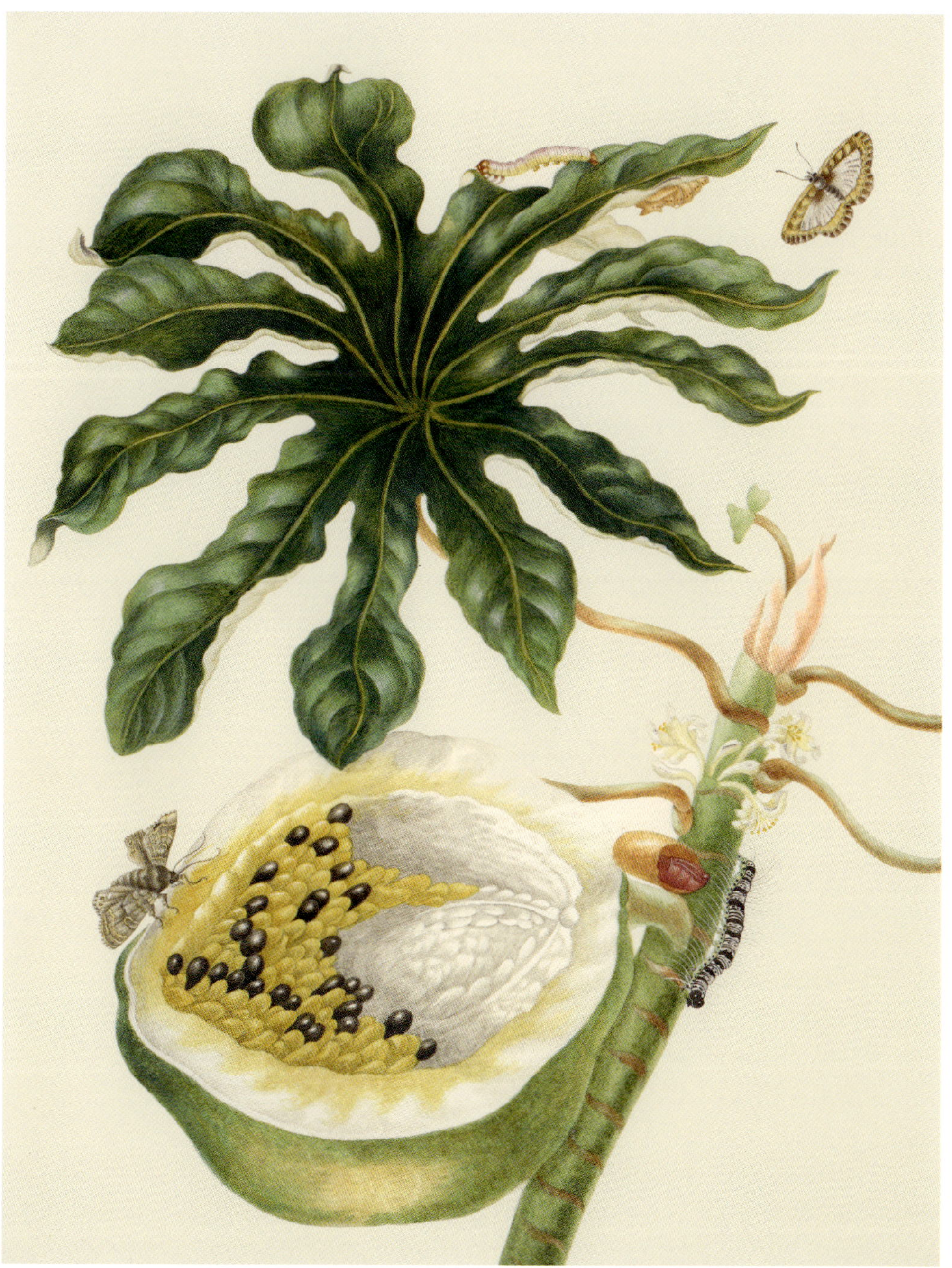

OPPOSITE

Auriculas
Alexander Marshal,
*c.*1650–82

RCIN 924281

Tree hibiscus (detail)
Mark Catesby,
*c.*1722–6

RCIN 926052

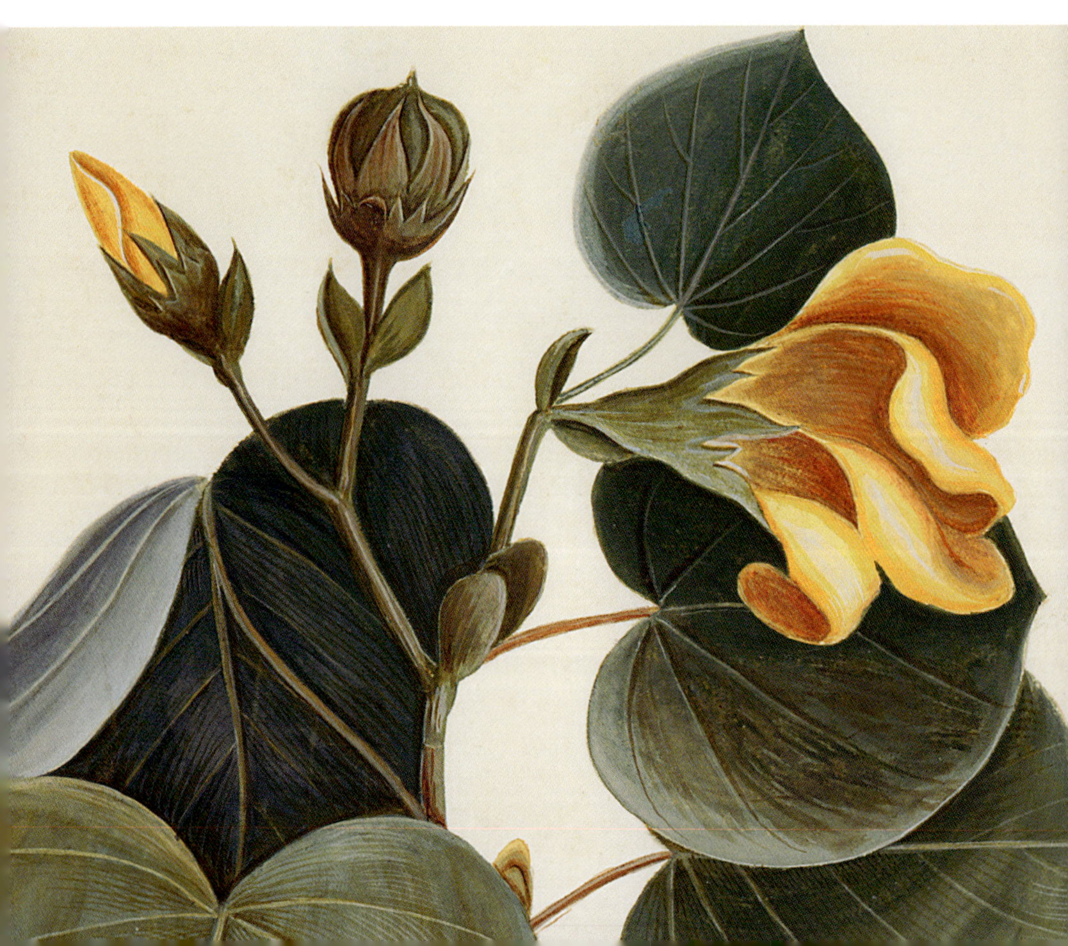

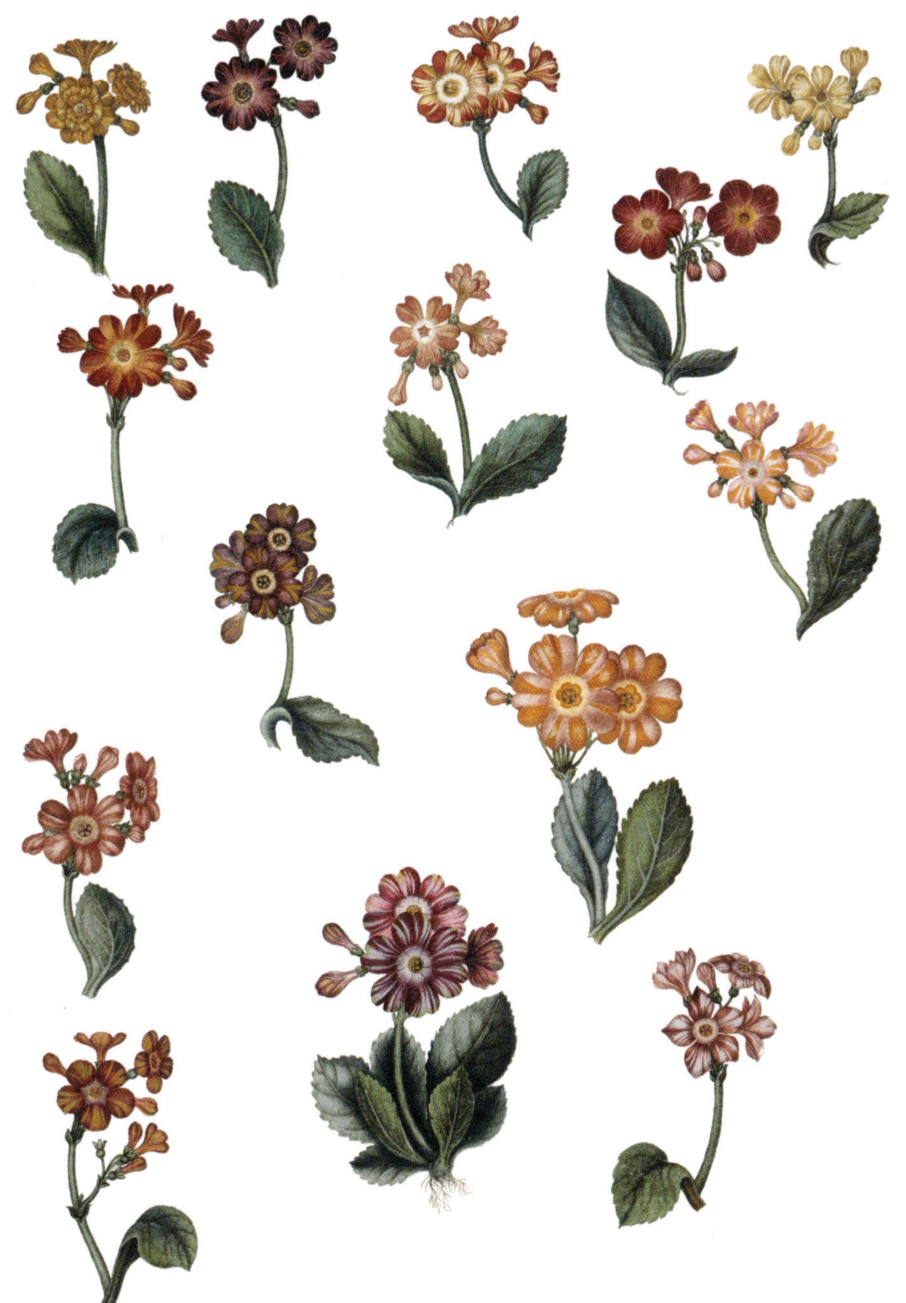

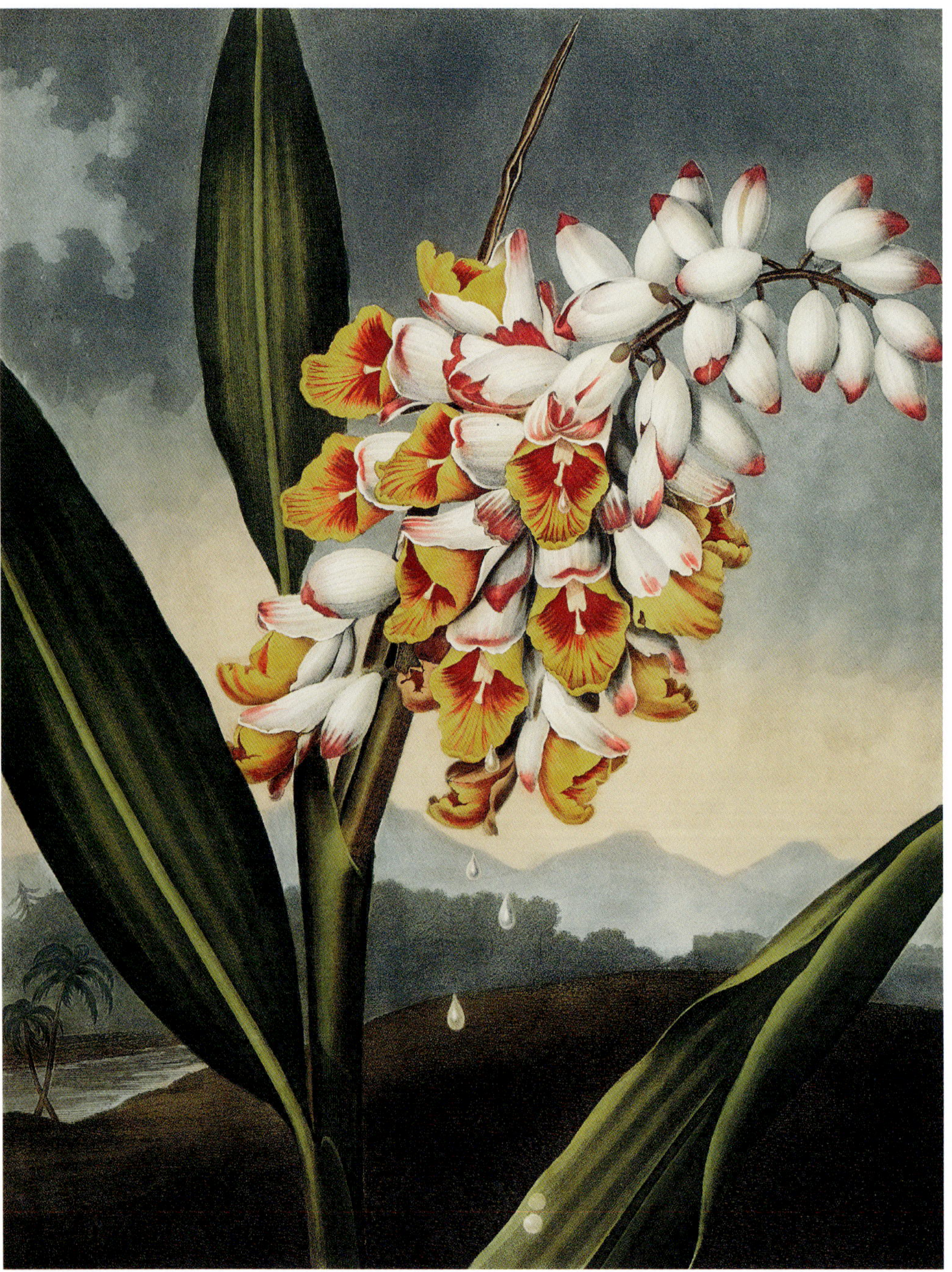

The nodding renealmia

From Robert John Thornton, *Temple of Flora*, 1807

RCIN 1059578

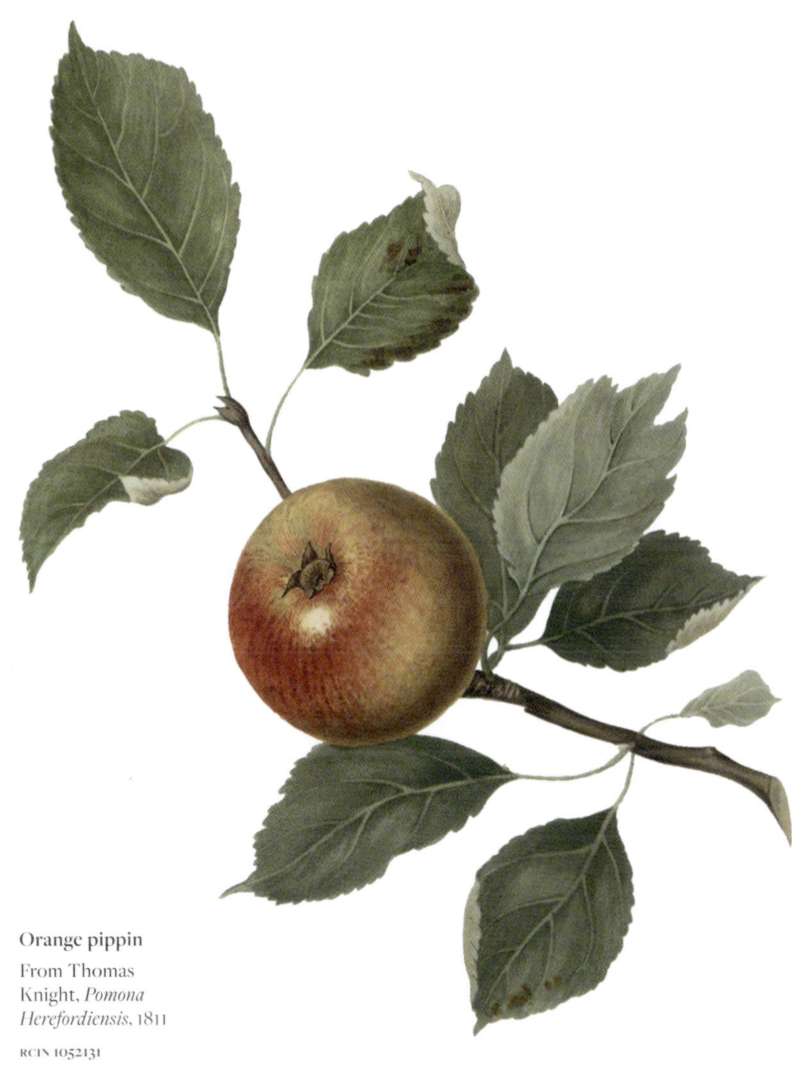

Orange pippin

From Thomas Knight, *Pomona Herefordiensis*, 1811

RCIN 1052131

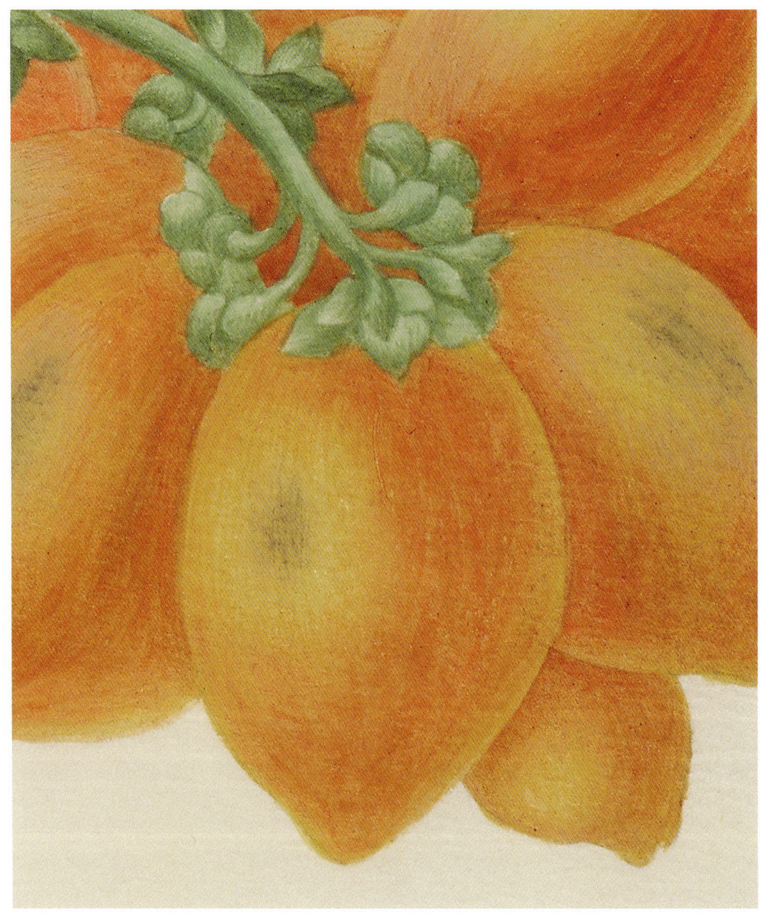

**Yellow mombin
(detail)**

Maria Sibylla
Merian 1702–3

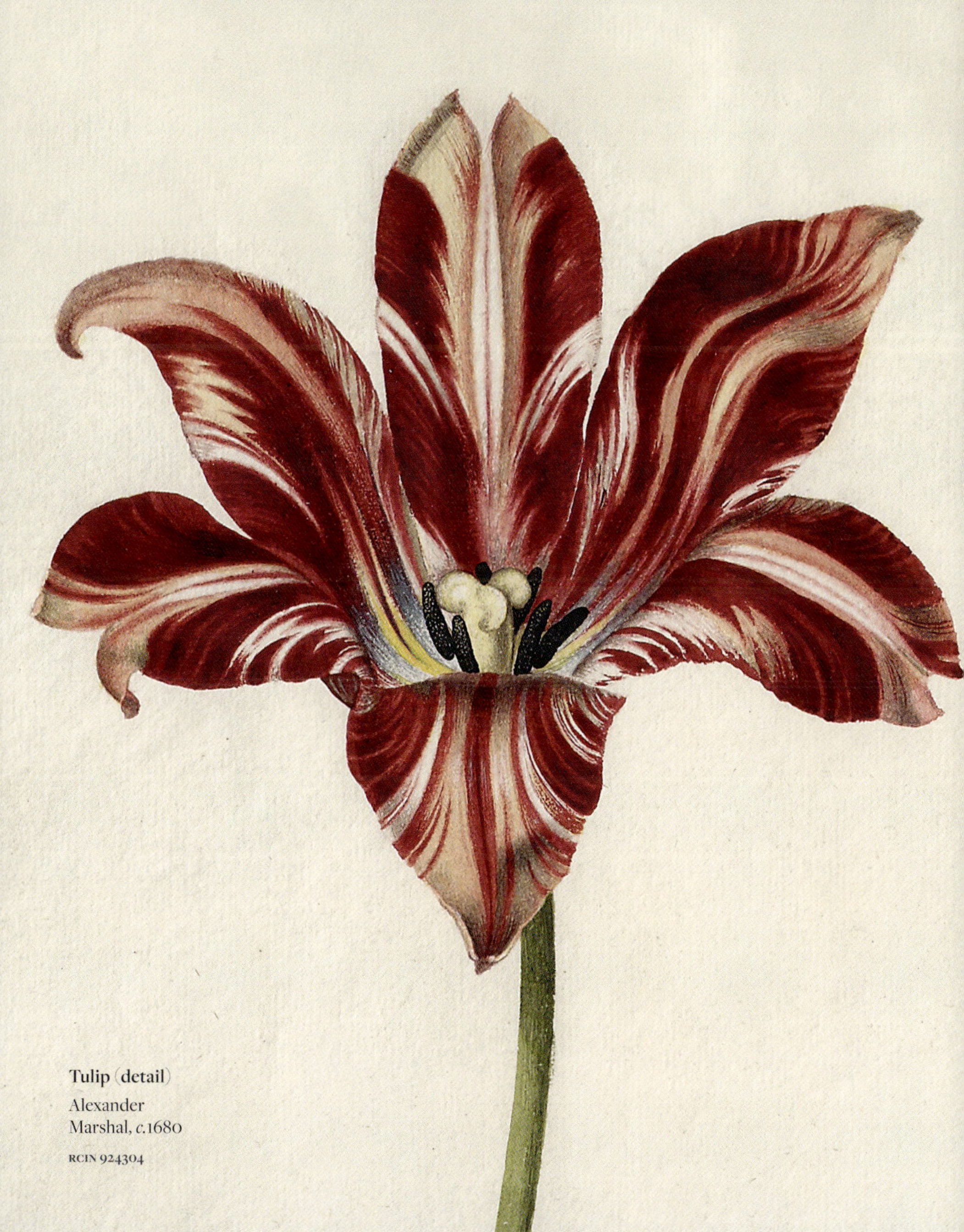

Tulip (detail)

Alexander
Marshal, *c.*1680

RCIN 924304

Further Reading

David Attenborough *et al.*, *Amazing Rare Things: The art of natural history in the age of discovery*, 2007

David Freedberg and Enrico Baldini, *Citrus Fruit*, 1997

David Freedberg, *The Eye of the Lynx*, 2002

Fabio Garbari and Lucia Tongiorgi Tomasi, with introduction by David Freedberg, *Flora: The Erbario Miniato and Other Drawings*, 2007

Kate Heard, *Maria Merian's Butterflies*, 2016

Prudence Leith-Ross with contributions by Henrietta McBurney, *The Florilegium of Alexander Marshal in the Collection of Her Majesty The Queen at Windsor Castle*, 2000

Henrietta McBurney, *Illuminating Natural History, The Art and Science of Mark Catesby*, 2021

Maria Sibylla Merian (ed. by Marieke van Delft and Hans Mulder), *Metamorphosis insectorum Surinamensium*, 2016

Amy R.W. Meyers and Margaret Beck Pritchard, *Empire's Nature, Mark Catesby's New World Vision*, 1999

E. Charles Nelson *et al.*, *The Curious Mr Catesby*, 2015

David Pegler, David Freedberg, *Fungi*, 2006

James L. Reveal, 'Identification of the plants and animals illustrated by Mark Catesby for his *Natural History of Carolina, Florida, and the Bahama Island*', *Phytoneuron*, 2013

Bert van de Roemer *et al.*, *Maria Sibylla Merian, Changing the Nature of Art and Science*, 2022

Elisabeth Rücker and William T. Stearn, English translation of Maria Merian's *Insectorum Surinamensium*, 1982

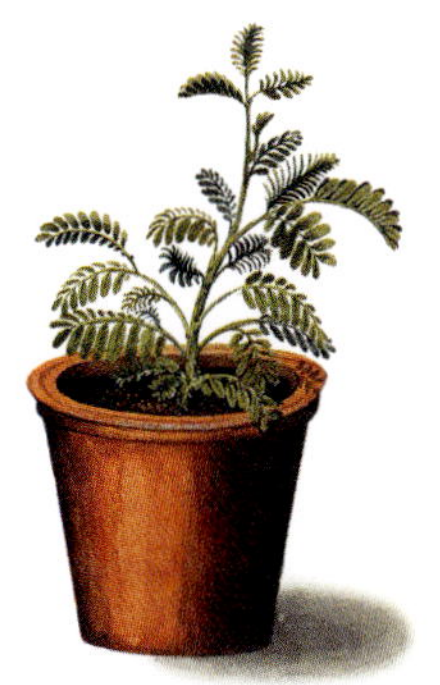

Humble plant
Alexander Marshal,
*c.*1650–82

RCIN 924410

Discover more prints and drawings in the Royal Collection at **www.rct.uk/collection**

Published 2025 by Royal Collection Trust
York House, St James's Palace
London SW1A 1BQ

© Royal Collection Enterprises Limited 2025 |
Royal Collection Trust

Introduction by Alice Alder, Assistant Curator of Prints
and Drawings, Royal Collection Trust

Unless otherwise stated all text and images are
© Royal Collection Enterprises Limited 2025 |
Royal Collection Trust

ISBN 978-1-909741-93-5

104666

10 9 8 7 6 5 4 3 2 1

A catalogue record of this book is available from the
British Library.

Designer: Matthew Wilson | www.mexington.co.uk
Concept design: Jevon Hall
Publisher: Kate Owen
Commissioning Editor: Anjali Bulley
Managing Editor: Polly Fellows
Production Manager: Sarah Tucker
Reproduction: DL Imaging
Printed on GallerieArt Matt 150gsm
Printed and bound in Slovenia by DZS Grafik

Royal Collection Trust publications
are distributed in North America by
The University of Chicago Press,
1427 East 60th Street, Chicago,
IL 60637 USA (press.uchicago.edu),
and throughout the rest of the world
by **Thames & Hudson Ltd.**,
6–24 Britannia Street, London
WC1X 9JD (thamesandhudson.com).

EU Authorised Representative:
Interart S.A.R.L.
19 rue Charles Auray,
93500 Pantin, Paris, France
productsafety@thameshudson.co.uk
interart.fr

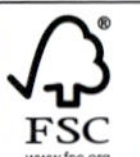

Broccoli

Collection of Cassiano
dal Pozzo, c.1650

RCIN 921143

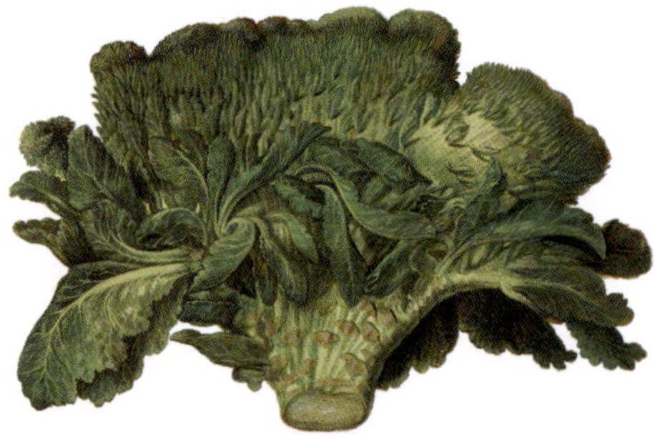

FRONTISPIECE

Tulips

From Robert John
Thornton, *Temple of
Flora*, 1807

RCIN 1059578

TITLE PAGE

Cherries

Alexander Marshal,
c.1680

RCIN 924424